PLAY FOOTBALL

A GUIDE TO TECHNIQUES & SKILLS

STEVE ROSSITER

Foreword by
BRUCE GROBBELAAR

Illustrated by Hugh Raine
Graphic design by Richard Blyth

Published by

MELROSE BOOKS

An Imprint of Melrose Press Limited
St Thomas Place, Ely
Cambridgeshire
CB7 4GG, UK
www.melrosebooks.com

FIRST EDITION

Cover designed by Richard Blyth

ISBN 978-1-906050-16-0

Printed and bound in China by:
1010 Printing International Limited.

CONTENTS

FOREWORD

It is an honour to be asked to write the foreword to this book. When I started in football in 1974 I did not have the benefit of access to a manual such as this to set me on the right path, but, for budding footballers of today, here is a book that will most certainly assist them to acquire the skills and broaden their knowledge of the 'beautiful game' and I am pleased to be associated with it.

After my 29 year career as variously player, coach and manager in the football leagues of Canada, England and South Africa, I had the opportunity to travel through Africa, where I visited schools in several different countries. It was during this time that I saw first-hand a huge enthusiasm for the game, but somewhat tempered by an extreme shortage of equipment and facilities. With the publication of this manual, however, I believe there is now an accessible resource that can be a huge benefit in these areas, as well as the better financed schools and clubs. Anywhere in the world in fact, as the extensive use of clever illustration extends the use of this book beyond the English reader.

Football is a team game that relies on individual technical skills, and the techniques need to be mastered by each player before the team can play at its best. The author and illustrator have done a fine job of producing an informative and instructive coaching manual which can be used by anyone starting out in the game, irrespective of their age! Read this manual, absorb the lessons, then practise, practise, practise … but above all, enjoy!

Bruce Grobbelaar
627 games for Liverpool FC (1981-94)
Liverpool playing record – 1 European Cup, 6 League Titles, 3 FA Cups, 3 League Cups
46 full Internationals playing for Zimbabwe
Manager in South African Premiership

INTRODUCTION

That comfortable control and teamwork seen in professional football is stunning to watch. It looks easy when a player controls the ball in an instant, plays a one-two accurately with a teammate before moving into the opponent's penalty area and unleashing a goal scoring shot. Each step in that magical action is made up of ball techniques and skills which you can learn too.

With sound technical ability you can enjoy the game, contribute to the team and grow in self confidence. This book introduces and explains the ball techniques which can form the foundation for your football skills.

Each technique and skill is presented using words, images and exercises so you can read how it's done, see how it's done and practise it.

There are many demonstrations and training exercises for you to enjoy while learning, practising and honing your ball skills.

The routines are suitable for solo, one to one and multi player activities, which allow football techniques to be learnt together at training and reinforced at home. The group training is oriented about a junior football team.

Football is a skilled, technical, team game but it all starts with you and a ball.

INTRODUCTION

Meet the junior football team players taking part in the demonstrations, exercises and games throughout the book.

Ryan	Katie	Jay	Oscar	Emily	Aiden

Tom	Molly	Sam	Zack	Mary	Callum

THE PLAYERS IN THE 'PLAY FOOTBALL' TEAM

BALL CONTROL AND KICKING

First of all it starts with you just kicking the ball around. It's good fun. If you kick the ball against a wall it bounces back, if you kick a ball in the air it comes down and if you kick the ball in open space you can chase it and catch it up. But how do you kick the ball against a wall so it comes straight back to you? How do you keep the ball in the air repeatedly without it touching the ground? How do you run with the ball at your feet and keep it under control? These are questions that soon enter your mind and it's not always easy to fathom out the answer.

If you're looking to just kick around in the park or play in a team it's still interesting to know how to do certain things with the ball. The better you get at control the more time and space you will have to kick the ball. The better you get at kicking then each kick will be more accurate and productive.

It gives great satisfaction to be able to bring the ball under control and pass it to where you want. If you can work towards mastering control and kicking to a level where you feel comfortable on the ball and enjoy possession, then the world of football will open up to you.

It's not easy and it may take years to be proficient, so be patient because you can do it.

CONTROL AND KICKING AREAS OF THE FOOT

Different parts of the foot are used for different types of kick. The descriptions used in this book for the control and kicking areas of the foot for specific types of kick are shown below.

Top of foot. Bony arched area at top of foot. Used for powerful low or lofted drives like shots, crosses, corners, clearances and long passes.

Also used for spinning passes and shots or for control and running with the ball.

Inside of foot or side foot. Large area at side of foot. Used for control, very accurate short passes on the ground and when dribbling.

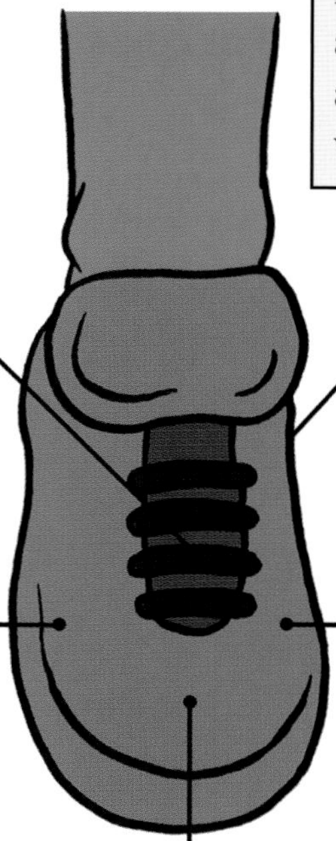

Outside of foot. Area around little toe metatarsal. Used for control, dribbling and running with the ball. Also used for spinning passes and flicks. Less powerful than top of foot or ridge of big toe kicks.

Ridge of big toe or ridge. Bony area of big toe metatarsal where it joins the big toe. Used for accurate and quite powerful lofted kicks such as floated drives, chips and crosses. Also used for spinning passes and shots or when dribbling and running with the ball.

Top of toes. Area where metatarsals meet toes. Used for close control when dribbling and running with the ball. Can be used to chip or flick the ball into the air.

The word instep is often used to describe a kicking area of the foot but seems to identify different areas to different people and leads to confusion. To avoid confusion the word instep is not used in this book.

CONTROLLING THE BALL

Control a ball on the ground

Side foot control

Controlling the ball with the inside of your foot, or **side foot**, is the single most used technique in football. So it's a great skill to master.

Contact zone on the ball

The contact zone on the ball for side foot control is in the middle, where the horizontal and vertical centre lines cross.

Contact zone on the foot

The contact zone on the foot for side foot control is in the large middle area of the inside of your foot away from the heel and toes.

Right foot side foot control contact zone.

Left foot side foot control contact zone.

Side foot control technique

To be able to control the ball your whole body needs to be balanced and comfortable with your controlling leg knee bent and your foot turned out at right angles. To take the pace off the ball and make it stop at your feet, make contact with the ball and deliberately move your foot back to cushion the ball to absorb its energy. Bring your foot and the ball to a halt together.

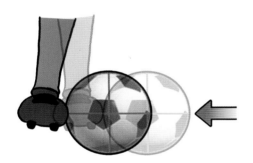

Side on view of foot, making contact, yielding and cushioning the ball to a stop.

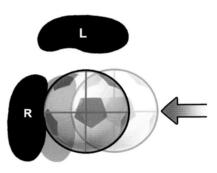

View from above showing initial contact on ball, then the foot moving back to bring the ball and foot to a halt together.

Keep your eye on the ball

Always keep your eye on the ball at the moment when you make contact to control the ball.

Ryan has his eye on the ball when it gets close so that the correct part of his foot makes contact with the ball for good control. He'll judge his timing to bring the ball to a halt better too.

Molly demonstrates controlling the ball to a halt

To bring the ball to a halt at your feet when it is passed directly to you on the ground, try this like Molly.

Molly adjusts the position of her feet so the foot being used to control the ball is in line with the motion of the ball.

Molly turns her side foot out at right angles to face the ball with her foot off the ground and level with the centre of the ball.

When the ball makes contact with her foot Molly lets her foot yield and go backwards a bit to cushion the ball bringing the ball to a halt at her feet.

Jay and Ryan practise side foot control

The more you practise side foot control the less distance your foot will travel to cushion the ball to a standstill.

Jay and Ryan practise side foot control using one ball and passing it backwards and forwards to each other. They cushion it to a halt each time they receive the ball.

Jay and Ryan hold their bodies well balanced and in a comfortable position when controlling or playing the football. They keep their feet no more than shoulder width apart and use their arms for good balance.

The yielding of their controlling foot is almost imperceptible now.

Practise control with both feet because the ability to control the ball with either foot gives players a big advantage in competitive football.

Having difficulty with the side foot control?

If you're trying to control the ball to a halt and the control isn't coming off as you intended, the reason may be one of the following :-

Problem	Solution
Pass to you is wide	Move across to meet the ball and get behind the line of its movement for good contact and control. Avoid overstretching.
Ball bounces off ankles, toes or side foot away from you	Keep your eye on the ball.
	Bend your knee and ensure foot contact is in the centre of the ball and not too high or low or wide.
	Make sure your foot is turned out at right angles to the line of movement of the ball.
	Get the timing right so your contact with the ball can cushion it to a standstill.

Control the ball to the side

Bringing the ball to a halt demonstrates an understanding of basic ball control. From this position you can touch it a second time to the side ready to pass. Alternatively you could play the ball with your first touch; that is one touch to where you want it ready to pass. Achieve this by cushioning and redirecting the ball in a single movement without letting the ball stop. It saves time and prevents opponents rushing in with a tackle.

First touch control ready to pass exercise

Relax your foot, like Katie, so it recoils and absorbs some of the football's energy on contact and rotate your foot towards the direction you want the ball to go. Depending on the angle your foot makes contact with the ball, it should rebound off your foot and move forward and to the side to the desired position ready for kicking.

Katie receives a pass on her right foot and angles her foot so the ball rebounds gently across her body.

With one step to get her standing foot in position she can pass the ball left-footed to a teammate.

Control a ball in the air

Cushion a bouncing ball

The ball sometimes comes to you in the air. As long as you can get a foot to the ball the control is easiest to achieve with the side foot.

The ball is bouncing towards Jay so he bends his knee and lifts his controlling left foot higher in the air to make contact with his side foot on the ball. He cushions the ball to the ground to gain control.

You're making it look easy, Jay.

Timing is crucial to good ball control.

Cushion a high ball

If the ball comes to you out of the sky, the simplest and most successful method of controlling the ball is again to use your side foot.

Jay sees the ball coming at him from a defender's high clearance so he positions himself so he can get his right side foot directly under the ball as it comes down.

Jay lets his foot give way on impact to cushion the ball gently to the ground at his feet.

That's a very difficult control.

Well executed, Jay.

You could also use the top of your toes to cushion the ball but its narrow contact surface means there is more risk of the ball skidding away beyond your reach.

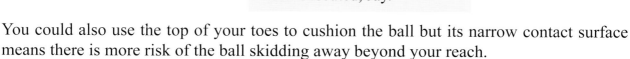

Chest Control

If the ball is coming from a height and will reach you at about chest level then you can use your chest to cushion the ball. Your chest is a large area to control the ball with. Lean back, flex at the knees and hips to allow your chest to cushion the ball and then push it straight up into the air. This lets gravity absorb the energy in the ball and drop it nicely at your feet.

Ryan sees a high looping clearance from the opposition coming straight at him and with no one to head it to he decides to control it with his chest.

He gets slightly under the ball, leans back a little and on contact cushions the ball deliberately straight up into the air just in front of himself.

The ball falls at his feet and Ryan is ready to start a counter attack.

Good timing, Ryan.

If the ball is coming faster and flatter to you at chest level then you can cushion the ball straight to the ground with your chest like Oscar.

Oscar sees the ball coming straight at him so he puffs his chest out and leans slightly forward.

On contact Oscar yields, cushions the ball and redirects it straight to the ground.

The ball bounces up a bit but Oscar uses his foot to quickly gain control.

That's amazing control, Oscar.

With each of these chest control techniques the ball can be chested either forward or left or right depending how you present your chest to the ball to redirect it.

Thigh Control

An alternative to side foot control and chest control for a high or bouncing ball is thigh control. Use the top of your thigh away from your knee because it's larger, softer and will cushion the ball more.

Molly anticipates a high clearance and runs towards it. As she gets there she decides to control it using her thigh.

She positions herself under the flight of the ball and lifts her knee off the ground. The ball makes contact with her thigh muscle between her hip and knee and …

… just like with side foot control, she lets her thigh yield on impact to cushion the ball to the ground.

That's magic, Molly.

Molly practises thigh control by gently throwing the ball into the air and controlling it with her thigh on the way down. She cushions the ball to the ground and controls it many times until she is comfortable using the thigh control technique with either leg.

KICKING THE BALL

Kick a ball across the ground

To kick the ball across the ground and keep it at ground level hit it no lower than the middle.

Side foot pass

Let's start with the side foot pass. This is the most common type of pass especially for short distances at ground level. It's quite easy to execute and very accurate.

Contact zone on the ball

Contact is made with the side foot (inside of the foot) onto the centre or middle of the ball, as in side foot control.

The contact zone on the ball for a side foot pass is in the middle, where the horizontal and vertical centre lines cross.

Contact zone on the foot

The contact zone on the foot is the **side foot**.

Right foot side foot pass viewed from the front.

Left foot side foot pass viewed from the front.

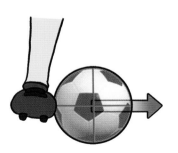

Right foot side foot pass from the side.

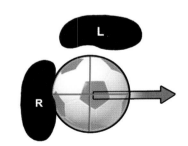

Right foot side foot pass from above.

Side foot kick technique

The side foot kick is struck with the side foot onto the middle of the ball. To be able to kick the ball and control the pass your whole body needs to be balanced and comfortable during your approach, set up for the kick and during the kick and follow through. Your standing foot, placed beside the ball, gives your body stability while your kicking foot is used for contact and the follow through to give distance and direction. Keep your eyes on the ball at the moment of contact and use your arms to help stay balanced. Your arm on the kicking foot side will naturally swing backwards as your kicking foot swings forwards.

BALL CONTROL AND KICKING

Emily demonstrates the side foot pass

Emily is practising side foot passes so she steps up to the ball facing towards the receiver…

… places her standing foot beside the ball and draws back her kicking foot, keeping her eye on the ball.

Emily bends her knee and turns her foot out at right angles and kicks through the ball with her side foot on the centre of the ball.

Throughout the contact she keeps her foot positioned at right angles to the direction the ball is to travel.

Emily follows through with the kicking foot in the direction of the player she is passing to.

Only after the ball has left her foot does Emily raise her head to see the action.

Well done, Emily, that's an accurate well weighted pass.

Ensure the weight or pace of the pass is appropriate for the distance the ball is to travel. This means the pass must be played firmly enough to reach the receiver but not so firmly that it is difficult to control.

Having difficulty with the side foot pass?

If the side foot kick isn't coming off as you intended, ask yourself why? It may be one of the following :-

Problem	Solution
Pass goes left or right of the receiver	Strike the ball with your side foot to avoid clipping it with your toes or heel.
	Foot should be turned out at right angles to the line of the pass.
	Follow through in the direction of the intended pass.
	Ensure your standing foot is close enough to the ball.
Pass goes through the air	Foot may be striking ball too low down so make sure you strike the ball in the middle.
Pass bobbles	Foot may be striking ball too high up so make sure you strike the ball in the middle.
Ball is too close to your feet to kick cleanly	Play or 'dig' the ball out into the open then step up to it and pass.

Remember, when you've seen where you are going to pass, keep your eyes on the ball throughout the back lift, contact and initial follow through until it is clear of your foot. Then look up to see what's happening.

Side foot control and passing

Passing and control are closely linked and the greater the variety of control and pass techniques you can call on then the greater your chances of making a successful pass in any particular situation. Like Katie earlier you can, with your first touch, control the ball across your body before passing it or you could develop the cushioned control into a one touch pass redirecting the ball straight to a teammate. Once these techniques are mastered you have achieved a high standard of ball control and passing.

Side foot control and pass practise

Mary practises side foot passing against a wall, or with a partner, kicking the ball with her left and right foot. Sometimes she controls the ball to a halt then 'digs' it out with the outside of her foot ready for passing with the same foot, or plays it, first touch, across her body with one touch of her side foot, before passing with the other foot. Mary sometimes passes the ball straight back to the wall with her first touch.

Mary digs it out and passes

Mary brings the ball to a halt with her right side foot.

To get the ball into the open and make a clean pass Mary moves her right foot to the left of the ball and plays it into space with the outside of her right foot.

Mary takes one stride and then plays the ball sweetly to the wall.

Mary's one touch and pass

Mary moves across to receive the ball on her right foot …

… and with one touch side foot controls it across her body …

… then takes one stride and passes it left-footed back at the wall.

Mary's learning quickly that the ball can be controlled in many different ways before the pass is made.

One touch side foot control and pass exercise

Here Callum and Emily pass the ball to and fro around a cone. After each pass they must move to the other side of the cone. The receiver must control the ball and move it sideways, first touch, beyond the cone and then, taking only one stride if possible, pass it back.

Callum passes the ball right-footed to Emily. Emily, balanced and mobile, gets behind the line of the ball ....

… to cushion and redirect it left-footed sideways, across her body, to the right of the cone with one touch.

Emily takes one stride after the ball while Callum sidesteps left to receive the pass.

Emily places her standing left foot beside the ball and side foots the ball right-footed to Callum. Emily immediately starts moving left, back to the other side of the cone while Callum prepares to cushion the ball left-footed onto his right foot again.

You're both light on your feet and well balanced.

Emily and Callum pass the ball right-footed to each other anti-clockwise around the cone for about a minute. Then they change and pass and move the ball in a clockwise direction. The first touch cushion control is now right-footed and passes this time are left-footed.

Low drive

The drive is the most powerful kick available and will fly fast to its destination. The low drive, keeping the ball close to the ground, is used primarily in attack for shooting on goal. It can also be used to make fairly long distance penetrating passes but they risk being intercepted. The low drive will travel straight and quickly if struck precisely but can go astray if hit off centre. Steven Gerrard is brilliant with this kick when he shoots at goal.

Contact zone on the ball

The contact zone on the ball for a low drive is in the middle where the vertical and horizontal centre lines cross.

Contact zone on the foot

The contact zone on the right and left foot for a low drive is the hard bony **top of the foot** as shown below. Notice Molly's toes, heel and knee are in a straight line. The hard bony **ridge** of your foot can also be used to strike a low drive but it's not quite as powerful.

Front on view of right foot drive contact zone on top of foot.

Front on view of left foot drive contact zone on top of foot.

Low drive technique

The low drive is struck with the top of the foot onto the middle of the ball. Approach the ball from the side, place your standing foot beside the ball and to keep the ball low get your body forward and your kicking leg knee over the ball or in line with it on contact. Your toes, heel and knee are in a straight line so to get your foot through the kick, without scraping the ground, either raise yourself up onto your standing foot toes or bend your kicking leg knee or lean sideways. Follow through in the direction you want the ball to travel. The low drive is a powerful kick so use your arms to balance the strong force of the kick and follow through.

Ryan demonstrates the low drive

Notice Ryan leaning sideways in the picture on the left to allow his straight right leg with toes pointed down to drive through the ball without hitting the ground.

Ryan confidently shapes up to drive the ball at goal. His high backlift will generate power.

Here Ryan is more upright and bends his knee to get his foot through the ball without scraping the ground. Use your arms to balance the powerful force of the leg driving forward.

Having difficulty with the low drive?

Driven kicks are quite difficult to master but once you've mastered it your play will change forever. If you encounter any of the problems below, see if the solution offered helps.

Problem	Solution
Ball won't stay down near the ground	Get your body, particularly your knee, over the ball or in line with the ball at the moment of contact to prevent the follow through lifting the ball.
	Point your toes down and keep them down during contact with the ball.
	Strike the ball on the middle, not low down.
Ball veers left or right from intended line	Keep your eyes on the ball throughout the back lift, contact and initial follow through, until the ball is clear of your foot.
	Concentrate on striking through the centre of the ball with the top of your foot.
	Ease off the power until your timing is just right.
	Make a smooth and controlled back lift, strike and follow through. Avoid snatching at the ball.

Kicking a ball into the air

To kick the ball into the air hit it below the middle. If you want the ball to travel long distances the ball must be kicked into the air over defenders' heads so it can't be intercepted. If you hit the ball below its horizontal centre line it will tend to rise however you present your foot to it, but there are many subtle variations of kicks that loft the ball into the air. Lofted kicks range from kicks that leave the foot like a cannon ball through spinning passes to delicate floated passes.

Lofted drive

The drive is the common term for the most powerful kick available and the lofted drive gets the ball in the air and covers long distances fast. It can be used for shots, corners, clearances or long passes like crosses. The elevation is quite easy to achieve but you've got to practise a lot to make this pass accurately. Lofted drives travel distances from 20m to 50m plus.

Contact zone on the ball

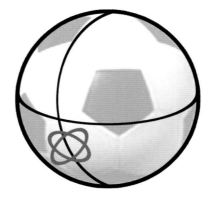

The contact zone on the ball for a lofted drive is on the vertical centre line below the horizontal centre line.

Contact zone on the foot

The contact zone for a lofted drive is directly on the hard bony **ridge** or if you roll your foot to point towards the direction of the kick then the **top of the ridge** or the **top of the foot** can also be used. The ridge and the top of the foot are the hard bony areas of the foot used for powerful kicks. Notice Katie's heel is turned inwards towards her other leg.

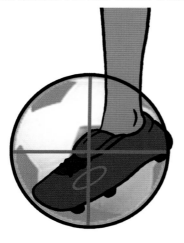

Front on view of right foot contact zone on the ridge for lofted drive.

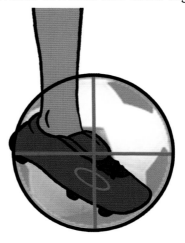

Front on view of left foot contact zone on the ridge for lofted drive.

Lofted drive technique

The lofted drive is struck with either the ridge, top of the ridge or top of the foot onto the area below the middle of the ball. Approach from the side, place your standing foot slightly wide of the ball and with a long back lift of the kicking foot sweep your leg powerfully through the ball and complete the kick with a long follow through. Follow through in the direction you want the ball to travel. Use your arms to balance the force of the kick and follow through.

Oscar and Ryan demonstrate the lofted drive

Oscar steps up to the ball and places his standing foot beside the ball and after he bends his kicking leg knee to get good back lift for the kick he drives through the ball to get lift and distance.

You can see Oscar from the side confidently hitting a lofted drive. In this instance he's making contact with the top of his foot below the middle of the ball. While he has contact with the ball his long follow through is aimed at his target.

Oscar's lofted drive will travel a long way over the heads of the defenders.

Ryan has controlled the ball and moved it out to the left so he can step up to it and send the ball up field to a teammate over the heads of defenders.

Here we can see Ryan hitting the left-footed lofted drive from the front. Notice his eyes on the ball and arms out for balance. His heel is turned inwards so he can make good contact below the centre of the ball with the ridge of his foot to get lift and make an accurate pass. His follow through will aid distance and direction.

Lofted drive - Cross from the wing

The cross is a special and important use of the lofted drive. The attacker is usually running with the ball and the cross will change the ball's direction dramatically. You will probably be shaping up at right angles to the direction of the intended kick so it is a difficult kick to deliver.

Callum is running with the ball at his feet down the right wing.

He looks up and sees Zack running into the penalty area so he decides to cross the ball. He plants his standing left foot close behind the moving ball ready for the pass.

Callum knows where he's going to kick it so he keeps his eyes firmly on the ball and swings his kicking right leg to make contact on the side of the ball, just below the middle, with the ridge of his foot, and follows through all the way across his body. The ball flies fast over the defenders into the penalty area, just as Callum intended.

Good cross, Callum.

Having difficulty with the lofted drive?

If the lofted drive isn't working due to one of the following problems perhaps the solution offered will help.

Problem	Solution
Ball doesn't rise	Make sure contact with the ball is below the middle of ball.
	Increase back lift and follow through to get more power into the kick.
	Contact with ball either too early or too late in sweep of kicking leg. Adjust standing leg position so low point of sweep occurs at contact with ball.
Ball doesn't travel far enough	This can happen, particularly for young players. Keep practising with a smaller and lighter ball until your timing and strength improve.
Ball pulls or slices to the side	Keep your eyes on the ball throughout the back lift, contact and initial follow through until the ball is clear of your foot.
	Make sure contact with the ball is on the vertical centre line of the ball.
	Follow through in the direction of the intended pass.

Floated drive

Floated drives are a variation of the lofted drive. They have less power than the lofted drive but more precision and are easier for the receiver to control. Examples of floated drive passes are crosses, corners and through balls intended to sit up for an attacker. The differences between a floated pass and a lofted drive are the pace and trajectory. A floated pass will travel slower and appear to hang in the air before it reaches its destination and then bounce higher when it lands. These differences are due to the ball being struck lower down and the angle the foot is presented to the ball on contact. Bobby Moore's pass to Geoff Hurst in the 1966 World Cup final for England's fourth goal is a classic example of a floated drive.

Contact zone on the ball

The contact zone on the ball for a long distance floated drive is on the vertical centre line below the horizontal centre line.

Contact zone on the foot

The contact zone on your foot for a long distance floated drive is towards the side of the **ridge** near the big toe. Notice how Sam's heel is closer to the ground and his foot turned out almost at right angles. It's turned out much more than with the lofted drive. He also gets lower under the ball to achieve the floating style of pass.

Right foot floated kick contact zone at the side of the ridge near the big toe.

Right foot floated kick contact viewed from the front.

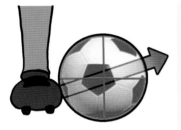

Right foot contact looking from the side.

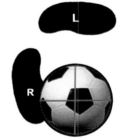

Right foot contact from above.

Floated drive technique

The floated drive is struck with the side of the ridge around your big toe onto the area of the ball well below the middle. Approach the ball from the side and place your standing foot far enough away from the ball to get your kicking foot through. From a fairly high backlift of your kicking leg, sweep your kicking foot, with your heel lower down and your foot turned out almost at right angles, through the ball. Follow through in the direction you want the ball to travel. Use your arms to balance the kicking forces acting on your body.

Zack and Ryan demonstrate the floated drive

Zack is shaping up well to hit a floated drive pass with his standing foot wide of the ball and a long back lift of his kicking foot.

Zack makes contact with the area around his big toe. His kicking foot is pointed out at right angles to the direction of the kick. His follow through will start off in the direction of his target until the ball has cleared his foot.

That was skilfully struck, Zack.

Ryan hits a good floated drive. Notice his eyes on the ball, arms out for balance and standing foot wide of the ball to allow his kicking leg through. He makes contact below the centre of the ball with the forward side of the ridge of his foot around his big toe to get lift and a long follow through to aid direction.

Zack and Ryan's long floated drive passes will loop through the air to their destinations and sit up when they bounce to help the receiving players' control.

Chip

Chip passes are used to achieve maximum height in the minimum distance. You may use a chip to get the ball up and over the goalkeeper if they have dived to the ground early or to pass through a line of defenders and make the ball stand up invitingly for an attacker to run on to.

There are two basic methods of achieving maximum elevation. The main method is played from the side with the kicking foot turned out at right angles to the direction of pass and making contact with the side of the ridge. The other method is played from over the ball with the kicking foot facing the direction of travel.

Contact zone on the ball

The contact zone on the ball for a chip played from either the side or front is on the vertical centre line low down near the bottom.

Contact zone on the foot

The contact zone on your right foot for a chip pass using both techniques is shown below.

Front on view of right foot contact zone using the side of **the ridge** near the big toe with the foot turned out. Notice Jay's heel is very close to the ground.

Front on view of right foot contact zone using the **top of your toes** with the foot facing forward.

Chip technique

The chip is a delicate pass to execute well and needs lots of confidence from the player. For both styles of chip your kicking leg has a short back lift and a minimal follow through. The ball is hit lower down and 'stabbed' to its destination.

Chip technique played from the side

Use the side of the ridge near your big toe with your foot turned out at right angles. Your foot gets as low under the ball as it can and sends it high into the air. There is minimal follow through.

Wayne Rooney often surprises goalkeepers with this chip from the edge of the penalty area.

Chip technique played from the front

Use the top of your toes to make contact. Your foot stabs under the ball sending it high into the air. There is no follow through. This method is not as commonly used because the direction and distance are difficult to control.

Molly and Sam demonstrate the chip pass

Molly and Sam want to practise chipping so they set up a hurdle to clear then stand on opposite sides and chip the ball to each other.

Molly takes one step from side on to the ball and with a short back lift brings her kicking foot down in a small arc to hit the ball low down.

Molly's follow through is very short so she hits the ball into the air with more height than forward momentum.

After a while Molly's got the chip off to a tee. You're talented, Molly, and determined.

Sam controls the ball to a halt and facing Molly stabs the ball back over the hurdle. Sam's foot stops almost as he hits the ball and it leaps into the air over the hurdle to Molly.

Well done, Sam. That's a very difficult chipping technique to master.

Volley

Kicking the ball when it is in the air is called a volley. It is a type of kick used most memorably in attacking situations when players are shooting at goal but it can also be used for defensive clearances and instant volley passes. A volley can be kicked with your side foot, ridge or the top of your foot.

For any volley, good contact and timing of the strike are of the essence to achieve control. These are difficult to manage on a ball moving towards you and need lots of concentration.

Attacking volley

For attacking volleys the ball direction of approach will determine which type of kick is used.

Contact zone for side on attacking volley

For a ball approaching from the side the contact zone is just above the centre or on the centre to keep the ball down and under the cross bar.

Just above the centre is safest because there's not much margin for error if you hit it on centre.

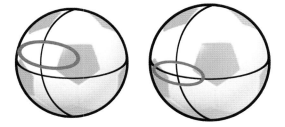

If the ball is coming from the left it is easier to volley with the left foot. Similarly, if the ball is coming from the right it is easier to volley with the right foot.

Mary demonstrates the side on attacking volley

Mary sees the ball being crossed from the wing. She quickly glances towards the goal to see where she wants to place the shot, then focuses on the ball and confidently leans sideways away from the ball and using the top of her foot redirects the volley to the corner of the goal she was aiming at.

Rather than giving it power Mary puts her effort into controlling the shot and redirecting it accurately so it doesn't rise over the bar. The power will automatically come from her well-timed contact on the ball.

What a good goal, Mary.

Contact zone for front-on attacking volley

For a ball approaching from the front the contact zone is in the middle just like a low drive. Make sure you keep control of the ball by pointing your toes down and getting your knee over the ball if it's possible.

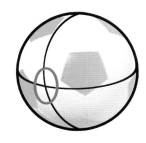

It's easier to get the timing right with the front-on volley but still concentrate on the control to keep it down below the cross bar.

Ryan demonstrates the front-on attacking volley

Ryan is about to volley the ball coming straight to him in the air. He's in the classic position with his body balanced, standing foot close, his knee bent over the ball and his eyes on the ball.

Ryan's concentration is total. This volley will fly like a bullet.

You could side foot either of the above attacking volleys for more accuracy but you would sacrifice power.

Defensive volley

For defensive volleys, like attacking volleys, the ball direction of approach will determine which type of clearance is used.

Contact zone for side-on defensive volley

For a ball approaching from the side the contact zone for a defensive volley clearance is just below the centre to get the ball in the air to clear the opposition.

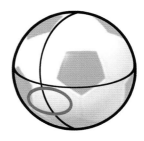

Mary demonstrates the side-on defensive volley

Mary has come back to help defend when a cross from the opposition comes to her.

Mary chooses to volley the cross clear. She leans sideways away from the ball and redirects the ball with the top of her foot making contact just below the middle so the ball rises safely. She doesn't snatch at the ball but times her contact perfectly.

Well cleared, Mary.

Contact zone for front-on defensive volley

For a ball approaching from the front the contact zone for a defensive volley clearance is on the vertical centre line just below the middle.

Callum demonstrates the front-on defensive volley

Callum is near his own penalty area, surrounded by opponents and the ball is bobbling in front of him, so he stands tall and making contact below the middle, uses the top of his foot and volleys the clearance up field.

He hits the ball low, but not under it, so it goes forward and not straight up and back down.

Half Volley

Half volleys are difficult kicks to time well and are not often used. They are generally executed from an upright stance as an instant kick on a ball landing at your feet. Hit the ball just as it touches the ground.

Jay demonstrates the half volley

Jay gently loops the ball into the air in front of him and as it lands and is still moving he drives through the ball making contact with the top of his foot. His toes are pointed down and the ball flies a few inches above the ground.

Spinning passes

Striking the ball off-centre or hitting the ball at an angle makes the ball bend or swerve off a straight line through the air or makes it move in a particular way off the ground when it bounces. You can kick a ball to make it spin left or right or give it topspin or backspin.

Spinning passes are complex varieties of all the basic 'straight' passes and are used by highly proficient players to get the ball round or over obstacles like defensive walls at free kicks or clever passes behind defenders or spectacular swerving shots.

The height of contact on the ball depends on whether you are going to keep the ball low or lofted. The amount of bend and the distance covered depends on the angle of contact. The more glancing the contact the more it will spin but the less it will travel. The straighter the kick the less it will bend but the further it will travel. Spinning passes are sometimes easier to perform if the ball is rolling towards you.

Bend the ball to the right

Strike across the ball with either foot from right to left. From above you can see the ball swing towards the right through the air. The standing foot is slightly behind the ball to allow the kicking leg through.

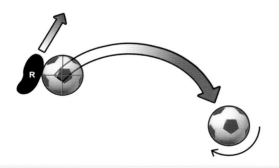

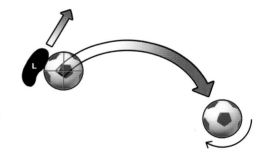

Outside of right foot contact with follow through going left.

Inside of left foot contact with follow through going left again.

Bend the ball to the left

Strike across the ball with either foot from left to right. From above you can see the ball swing towards the left through the air.

Inside of right foot contact with follow through going right.

Outside of left foot contact with follow through going right.

Topspin

To impart topspin to a kick, with the ball on the ground, the ball must be hit below the middle to make it rise but also the foot must be rising to make it spin. Contact is usually made with the side of the ridge near the big toe. It's very difficult to produce topspin successfully even for professionals. The most prominent example of topspin is a fast moving free kick over a defensive wall. In this case the ball must rise over the wall and then dip quickly to get under the cross bar and into the net. A straight forward lofted drive would rise over the wall but would not dip quickly enough. David Beckham has taken topspin and bending free kicks to a new level of accuracy.

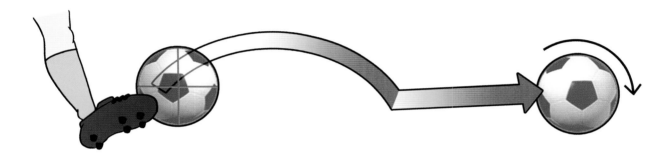

If a top spin ball hits the ground it will accelerate away.

Backspin

To achieve backspin the kick is similar to the floated drive and chip passes seen earlier. It is far easier to achieve backspin on a ball than topspin. Hit it low down with a short follow through.

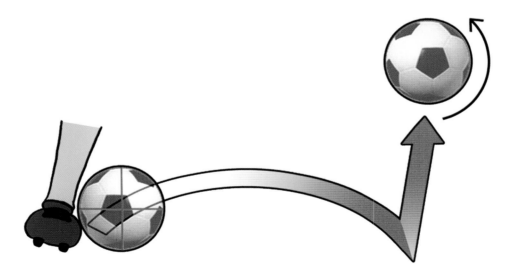

The ball will rise and come down quite slowly and when it bounces will tend to 'sit up' rather than accelerate away, so it is a good pass for an attacker to run on to.

Control and kicking exercises

Solo Keep Ups

Keeping the ball up in the air using your feet is a very important solo ball control skill. The more capable you are at keeping the ball in the air and under control then the better you are likely to be at controlling and passing the ball during match play. It is not necessary to be able to bounce the ball hundreds of times at one go because match play does not demand it but the instinctive and natural movement of the body to adjust to different tight ball control situations is necessary.

It takes two feet to keep the ball up, the kicking foot and the mobile standing foot. Get yourself relaxed and comfortable too.

It could be said that if after a couple of years' practise you can keep the ball up twenty times on either foot then you are on your way to having a firm foundation in the fundamentally important technique of ball control.

Bounce and Keep Up

| Here Ryan starts by bouncing the ball on the ground and then uses the top of his toes to keep the ball bouncing on his foot. | He's doing five keep ups on his right foot followed by five keep ups on his left foot. |

Hit the ball at the bottom with the flat part of your foot near your toes. With your foot horizontal the ball will go up in the air and straight down to your foot again. The harder you hit it the higher it will go. The ball will inevitably go off line at some point so keep yourself relaxed and your standing foot mobile to regain control. If you lose control don't stretch or snatch at the ball, move to it quickly but keep your body balanced and comfortable.

If you're a beginner don't worry if the ball bounces on the ground, keep going because you will get better.

Roll and Keep Up

With the ball static under her right foot out in front of her, Emily rolls the ball back towards herself.

As her foot falls off the ball she puts her foot under the ball and flicks it into the air to start the keep ups.

A variation on the solo roll and flick up is to either kick the ball against a wall or get someone to pass it to you and then you flick the ball from the ground into the air when it arrives.

Try these three **hot starts** to begin your keep ups

Hot start 1

Callum starts with the ball on the ground between his toes and forward of his ankles.

Callum brings his toes together quickly under the ball and as the ball pops up into the air he moves his body into position to start the keep ups with either his left or right foot.

Hot start 2

Oscar has found a new way to get started. So with the ball on the ground between his feet

He rolls the ball using his right side foot up the inside of his left leg to part way up his calf.

Then he quickly switches balance and flicks the ball up into the air with his left side foot to start the keep ups.

Well done, Oscar.

Hot start 3

Zack starts like Emily with his foot on the ball …

… but in this hot start Zack rolls it towards his other foot.

Quickly he switches balance and flicks the ball into the air.

Good skill, Zack.

Invent your own keep up hot starts or watch the professionals for inspiration and copy them. It's not just juggling for juggling's sake it's good ball control practise. It's good for confidence too.

As you get better use both feet. You could try for 10 keep ups on one foot immediately followed by 10 on the other or using alternate feet left, right, left, right.

Once you've mastered the basics of keep ups with your feet, try introducing some inside of foot and outside of foot touches, thigh keep ups or touches off your chest or head.

Control and kicking in pairs

Practise different types of kicks, side foot passes, lofted drives, low drives, floated drives, chips, volleys and spinning passes, in pairs with each player standing about 20m apart to start with. The receiving player should control the ball quickly and positively before taking their turn to pass the ball. Initially get the technique right for the particular type of kick then increase the power and distance.

Lofted kicks and one-two exercise

As players get more able three players can practise with two players about 20m apart and one in the middle. The two outer players pass to each other by lofting the ball over the head of the player in the middle. The receiving player should control the ball and pass it to the middle player who passes it back for the player to loft the moving ball. The player in the middle returns a straight pass to the outer player each time.

Jay, Aiden and Katie start the practise with Aiden passing the ball to Jay. Jay lofts the ball over Aiden's head to Katie.

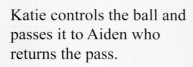

Katie controls the ball and passes it to Aiden who returns the pass.

Katie lofts the moving ball over Aiden's head to Jay for Jay to start again with a one-two to Aiden.

After a minute or so change the player in the middle. When you've had sufficient practise kicking with your favoured foot switch to your less favoured foot for a while.

Kicks and controls against a wall

Use a wall to practise different types of control and kicking.

Zack and Callum practise different kicks against a wall.

Zack wants to get better at volleying the ball and Callum wants to be able to spin the ball.

Good luck, you two.

Kicks and controls with a partner

Arrange yourselves into two groups of two about 25m apart with one ball between you. The idea is that one of you kicks the ball to the other two where one of them controls the ball and lays it off for their partner to kick it back to your group. The receiver of the kick in your team controls the ball and lays it off for the other player to kick back to the other two again. Repeat this exercise for as long as you like.

Here Zack and Callum get together as one group and Mary and Molly get together as the other group.

Mary starts and kicks the ball in the air to Zack.

Zack moves to get behind the line of the ball and chests it down to the side for Callum to control the ball and kick it back to Molly.

The four of them practise for ten minutes controlling and kicking the ball in different ways. It's an excellent way to improve your control and kicking.

Cushion control and passing exercise

The idea again is to reinforce one touch control and passing skills using both feet. Here the routine is to cushion the ball across your body with one foot and set up a pass for the other foot. How the ball gets from one foot to the other is for each of you to decide.

Form a triangle about 5m apart. Starting in an anti-clockwise direction each player controls the ball with one foot and passes with the other to the next player in the triangle.

Zack, Emily and Oscar form the triangle and Zack passes left-side-footed to Emily.

Emily cushions the ball with her right foot and redirects it onto her left foot with one touch and …

… side foots the ball left-footed to Oscar.

Oscar decides to backspin the ball with his right foot into the air ….

…. and gently volley the ball left-footed to Zack.

The players are becoming confident enough to use advanced skills when they practise and play. In this case Oscar's clever backspin and volley was totally in keeping with the one touch cushion and pass intention of the exercise. It's good to see them developing so well.

After a minute or so change the movement of the ball to the clockwise direction with the cushion control from the left foot to the right foot.

BALL CONTROL AND KICKING

Volley tennis

Practise aerial control and kicking in pairs with one of you on each side of a rail elevated about 40cm above the ground. The ball can bounce once and each of you can keep the ball in the air as many times as you want before passing it back to the other player. See how many times you can both get it over the rail.

Here Katie and Jay are practising their volley control and passing skills.

This is a difficult exercise to keep going but Katie and Jay are quite good at it. They move to get their bodies behind the line of each pass and control the ball with a deft touch.

There is no over stretching and snatching with these two.

Keep ups in pairs

This is a very advanced ball control practise. Working in pairs standing about 2m to 3m apart pass the ball to each other and keep it in the air using any ball control technique you want to practise. You can take any number of touches when it's your turn.

Sam bounces the ball to get started and side foot volleys it to Aiden. Aiden controls the ball with his chest and lets it drop to his thigh before touching it back to Sam. That's two.

Sam and Aiden control and pass the ball to each other using different techniques until the ball finally hits the floor.

Well done both of you, that was 10 passes without the ball touching the ground. That takes skill.

It's just like watching Brazil.

PASSING
AND MOVING

Passing and moving is the beating heart of football. It is the collective action of the individual players, which builds a strong team unit. Passing and moving uses the technical ball skills but also adds vision, support play, composure and attack to the common good. It is a shared vision between teammates to gain an advantage over opponents, hopefully leading to a shot on goal.

The last section identified the main ways of controlling and kicking a ball to get the right direction, distance and weight on the pass. This section will take those important techniques and link them to decision making and movement on and off the ball.

DEVELOP MOVEMENT

Passing during a game is control and kicking with more choice. More choice to select the right pass for the occasion and where and when to move. Passing and movement needs vision and communication too. Learning to keep your head up while keeping the ball in view is a must for the player in possession.

It takes at least two players to make a pass. One is the passer to select the receiver and the type and weight of pass and the other the receiver to make themselves available. Potential receivers also have to learn the new skill of finding space and showing for the pass.

Observe how play is developing

Keep your head up and notice everything that is going on. Try to see the big picture and the passing options, make your choice, then make the pass confidently and quickly. Keep the ball in your peripheral vision until you're about to play it. Listen for advice or calls from teammates to identify the best pass. When you play the ball remember, as always, keep your eye on the ball at the moment of contact.

Oscar has good vision of what's happening around him because he's got his head up and is using his eyes and ears to see teammates and listen for calls.

He can see where opponents and the ball are too.

Move after the pass

Initially, to comprehend and encourage the movement off the ball, we'll use exercises which require movement to a different position after the pass is made.

It is important to make your pass accurately so it reaches the receiver at the right height, direction and weight to give them the maximum chance of controlling the ball quickly. Passes on the ground are easiest to control. High passes will take more time to get under control.

Pass and move between lines exercise

For six or more players, divide yourselves into two rows facing each other 5m – 10m apart. The front player of one row passes to the front player of the other row then follows the ball and runs to the back of the other queue. The receiver controls and passes the ball to the new front player on the other row then follows the ball and joins the back of the other row.

Jay starts the practise and passes to Sam at the front of the other queue then immediately sets off running to the back of the other row.

Sam controls the ball ready to pass while Jay is joining the queue behind Molly.

Sam passes to Ryan and runs to the back of the other queue behind Katie. They continue until everyone has had, say, 10 goes on their favoured foot then repeat the exercise using their weaker foot.

Establish control of the ball before you pass it. Control allows an accurate pass to a teammate but poor control will probably mean a poor pass and the receiver having to run metres off line to retrieve the ball. When you receive the ball either control and pass the ball in one movement, or control it to a halt before passing.

Pass and move triangle exercise

This is similar to the pass and move in a line routine but this time you are passing and moving round a triangle with 5m – 8m long sides. Divide into three groups with a group at each marker. The intention is that you must each change the direction of the ball's movement with good control before the pass and then move is made.

Ryan starts with the ball, passes it clockwise to Katie at the next marker and runs after the pass to join the back of Katie's queue.

Katie controls the ball across her body with her right foot and passes it left-footed to Aiden at the next marker and runs to join Aiden's queue.

Katie's pass rolls kindly to Aiden and he flicks it, first touch, right-footed to Sam and sets off to join the back of Sam's queue.

Start off in one direction, say clockwise, and then after a couple of minutes go anticlockwise. Try using both feet when you receive the ball, one to control and the other to pass, unless like Aiden you can make a successful first time pass.

As a variation you could pass to the player at the front of one queue but run to join the back of the other queue. If the ball goes clockwise, you go anti-clockwise.

Pass across a circle exercise

Form a small circle, say 8m diameter. One player starts with the ball, passes to another player across the circle and then follows the ball and moves to that position. The receiving player controls the ball, passes to someone else in the circle and moves to that position. The passes can be of any type, on the ground or in air. Call the name of the player you intend passing to.

Zack has the ball and passes to Molly.

Zack follows the ball to take Molly's place in the circle.

Molly controls the ball to a stop, looks up and calls 'Callum' and passes the ball to him and follows the ball to take Callum's place in the circle.

Callum shapes up behind the line of the ball and passes it first time to Oscar.

Keep the circle small because this is a skills practise, not stamina training.

To increase awareness and concentration introduce a second ball. It certainly makes you keep your wits about you.

Pass to the middle of a circle exercise

Again form a circle, say 20m diameter, with one player in the middle. One of the players on the circle starts with the ball, passes to the player in the middle and then moves to that position. The receiving player in the middle controls the ball and passes to any player on the edge of the circle and then moves to that position. The passes can be of any type, on the ground or in the air.

Katie has the ball, passes it to Molly in the middle and runs to take Molly's place.

Molly controls the ball turns with it at her feet and chips it to Emily and runs to Emily's position.

Emily passes to Katie, who is now in the middle, and runs to take Katie's place.

You get to control, pass and move twice in quick succession. When you are the player in the middle you could also practise pretending (feinting) to go one way and take the ball the other way before you pass.

Passing while on the move

Now that you've practised controlling the ball, passing it and then immediately moving, let's try moving to meet the ball and passing the ball while on the move. This skill is taking us closer to team play.

One–two pass practise

Form two rows of players about 10m apart facing each other. The front player of one row has a ball and passes it towards the lead player of the other row who moves to meet the ball, controls and passes it straight back to the first player who then passes it to the next player in the other row.

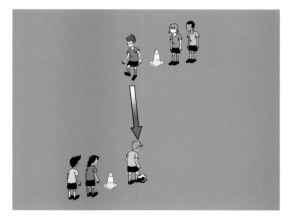

Zack moves forward with the ball and passes it towards Ryan.

Ryan moves to meet the ball and plays the one-two back to Zack.

Zack controls the ball and passes it to Katie then runs on to join her queue of players behind Jay.

Ryan joins the other set behind Molly and Oscar.

Katie continues the routine and prepares to make a one-two pass and move with Molly.

Time your movement to get yourself in line with the ball when it arrives so you can play it first time.

Pass and move in pairs practise

Passing the ball between two players who are both on the move in the same direction is good practise for control and passing. Here are two routines to help develop passing while on the move skills.

Freestyle one-two exercise

Aiden and Mary set off from one cone and pass the ball to and fro without any obstacles until they reach a second cone.

When they get to the second cone they turn and pass one-two to each other back to the first cone. They get practise using their left and right foot.

Obstacle one-two exercise

A more disciplined way to learn about moving in pairs with the ball is to set up some cones at about 3m intervals and pass the ball between the cones as you are moving forward.

Here Zack and Jay are at the front of their queues.

Zack sets off with the ball and runs with it to a little beyond the first cone where he passes it across to Jay.

Jay runs with the ball to a point a little beyond the second cone and passes it back to Zack.

They continue to the last cone then turn and go back to the beginning passing to and fro between the cones.

At the end they pass the ball to Sam and Oscar who take their turn to pass and move forward.

PASSING DECISIONS

In a competitive match there are constantly quick decisions to be made about moving to receive the pass and controlling the ball and making a successful pass. You have to decide who to pass to, what type of pass, what weight of pass, when and where to pass and after you've made the pass what do you do next. Choosing the right pass improves significantly with practise.

To whom and where should Mary pass? She's in full control of the ball and looking up so with the help of her teammates she'll make a successful pass.

What type of pass

Selecting what type of pass to make depends on the distance to be covered, the space available and the pace required. Where you are on the pitch and the proximity of defenders also has a bearing on your choice.

Long passes usually need to be lofted to prevent defenders from intercepting the ball. Short passes are better played on the ground.

The type of pass also depends on the space available and the chances of a teammate reaching the ball first. Short attacking passes in a congested area need to be accurate and to feet. If you're passing to a teammate moving forward into space put the ball in front of them so they can run onto it without breaking their stride. The attacking momentum is maintained too. Perhaps a chip pass through a surprised defence would be successful.

Weight of pass

Make the pass with the correct weight or pace so that the ball arrives at its destination and gives the receiver a good chance to control it. A short accurate pass to feet may be impossible to control if it is hit too hard. An over hit through ball may run harmlessly out of play and an under hit pass may be intercepted or it may invite a tackle. Try and make the receiver's life as easy as possible because that's what you'd want.

When and where to pass

Pass selection is a multiple choice decision and identifying the best passing option relies on quick thinking and good teamwork. Time the pass so it is successful; too early and the receiver may be marked; too late and they may stray offside.

Hopefully your teammates are moving and finding space to give you options so you can make a goal threatening pass or give it to a teammate in a better position. Don't pass to someone in a vulnerable position surrounded by opponents.

Here Aiden has two passing options either a sideways easy pass to Oscar or a more risky attacking through ball to Mary.

Because Mary is running into space and leaving her marker Aiden decides to pass to her. His accurate pass and her good running have made it into a worthwhile attacking move.

What to do next

After making the pass it is essential that you look around and move off the ball to find space. You're now a potential receiver of a pass.

Movement off the ball

The teammates of the player in possession have a massive responsibility. In a match every teammate is a potential receiver of the next pass. The more options the passer has the more likely your team is to retain possession so work together creating space and making yourselves available for a pass.

Aiden's teammates are working hard at running off the ball to find space for him to make a good pass.

Create space for yourself

If you can receive the ball in space you can be more creative than if you get the ball in a tight situation. Finding space is an important part of attacking play. There are several ways you can create space during a game. You could move on the blind side while your opponents are watching the ball or you could feint to run one way and go the other or you could get ahead of the defenders by gambling on where the pass will go before it is played.

Show for the pass

Make sure you are visible to the player in possession. Do not hide behind a defender as you will be difficult to pass to. Find space and show for the pass, perhaps call, put your hand up or point where you want the ball played.

If Sam stands in this position Molly wouldn't have an outlet for a pass.

But Sam finds space and the opening gives Molly a good opportunity to make a successful attacking pass.

Molly disguises the pass sometimes by feinting to pass one side of the defender to draw the defender off line before making the real pass to the other side.

Meet the ball

Beware of standing still as it can make you easy to mark. If the pass is made straight to you there may be a tendency to perhaps stand and wait for it to arrive. This may let a defender step in and intercept the pass because you can't see what's happening behind you. To avoid this, go to meet the pass.

Katie passes the ball to Oscar who can get to the ball first but should not stand and wait because the defender may step in.

Oscar moves forward to meet the pass and easily gets full possession.

Disguised run off the ball

You may not be the first receiver of a pass but still work to create space. Try a disguised run and change of direction feint.

Katie is in midfield with an opponent close by so to create space for herself she starts to run towards the left and as the defender turns to go with her …

…she quickly doubles back towards the right and creates yards of space to receive a pass.

Peel away from the defender

If you are being closely marked from behind, a way of creating space is to feint to go one way and then peel off in the other direction. The defender has to follow the first movement and will be left yards away when you receive the ball.

The defender is closely marking Callum so he feints as if to set off to go to his left taking the defender away.

Then Callum quickly doubles back and goes to his right creating lots of space to receive the ball.

Create space for others

When you're not in possession support the player who is in possession. Create space for others by occupying a defender's attention and freeing up space or perhaps make a dummy run to draw a defender away from a space a teammate can run into.

Lay the ball off

One way of creating space for a teammate is to draw the defender to one player who receives the pass with their back to goal and lays it off to a teammate who comes close for the pass.

Zack sees Oscar being closely marked on the edge of the opponent's penalty area and Jay running towards the penalty area, so to keep the defender away from Jay's run Zack …

… plays the ball to Oscar's feet and Oscar seeing Jay's run and signal lays the ball off for him to make an attacking run into the penalty area.

Clever move, you three.

Lay the ball off exercise

Form a 20m diameter circle with two in the middle this time. Pass to the first receiver who lays it off to the second player. The second player passes the ball out to a different player on the circle. The two in the middle adjust their positions so that when the ball is played back into the middle the first receiver controls it and lays it off to the second player. After thirty seconds swap the first and second receiver round. After a further thirty seconds swap the two players in the middle.

Jay and Ryan are in the middle. Zack plays the ball to Jay.

Jay lays the ball off to Ryan.

Ryan controls and turns with the ball and passes it to Callum. Jay faces Callum ready to receive the next pass.

Lay the ball off first or second touch because the quicker it's laid off the more surprising to the opposition and thus the more effective it is.

Run off the ball

If you can see a teammate moving into a potentially strong attacking position you could help them by running off the ball to draw defenders away and create more space for them.

Emily playing on the wing sees Katie moving forward with the ball and Molly the full back overlapping on the outside. Emily runs infield taking the defender with her so that…

… Katie's pass to Molly leaves Molly with lots of attacking space to use.

Emily's unselfish run has helped her team gain an advantage.

PASS AND MOVE AGAINST OPPONENTS

This is the first time that an opponent has been introduced to the routines. Now all your ball skills and passing and movement off the ball will be put to the test.

Introduce disguise into your passes. Disguising your intentions is an important part of the game because it gives you extra space and time. As you do when dribbling, fool the defender by feinting to pass one way and then pass the other. Perhaps look towards a space, or even point, before passing somewhere else.

Football is a permanently fluid game and passing and moving are the essence of good play. Pass and move exercises between two competing sides develop control, vision, fitness, positioning and teamwork.

A simple pass can become difficult once an opponent is there to disrupt your intentions.

Pass and move across a box exercise

One non contact way to practise getting the ball past defenders is to mark out an area about 8m square with one attacking player on each side of the square and two defenders inside the square. Each attacking player can move along the length of their side of the box but cannot enter the box. Each defender must stay inside the box.

The idea is for the attackers to pass a ball to each other across the box and keep possession. Keep the momentum up and the ball moving so the exercise is worthwhile. The defenders try to block or intercept the pass. If a defender knocks the ball out of the square they swap with the attacker who lost it. In any case swap the two defenders with two attackers after a minute or so.

Aiden, Ryan, Molly and Sam each patrol one side of the box while Callum and Katie play the defenders.

Sam starts with the ball and passes across the box to Ryan who is unmarked.

Ryan pretends to side foot the ball to Aiden fooling Callum into stepping right, leaving space for a neat pass to Molly.

Callum and Katie try to close Molly down quickly but Aiden, Ryan and Sam move to show themselves for Molly to choose a chip pass through to Aiden.

The square can be made bigger to accommodate more attackers and defenders or it can be made smaller to make passing harder.

3 v 1 exercise

Practise keeping possession and team play in a small zone about 10m x 5m with three attackers and one defender. There is more time on the ball for the attackers to control it and prepare for the pass. There are no goals or ends. The three attackers try to keep the ball by moving and passing to each other and the defender tries to intercept the ball and clear it out of the marked area. Physical contact is not allowed. Pass and move until the defender either clears the ball out of the play area or if the defender hasn't won the ball within a minute, the defender and one attacker should switch positions.

Katie, Molly and Zack form the starting attack while Callum is the first defender.

Katie passes the ball to Molly and Callum tries to close Molly down but it's not easy with two players available to pass to.

Molly feints to pass back to Katie but quickly passes to Zack. As Callum tries to block Zack's pass Katie and Molly move into positions where Zack can chose either of them to pass to.

Callum's finding it hard work but after a minute he swaps with Molly and takes his turn in the pass and move practise. The exercise can be adapted to suit 4 v 2 or other combinations of players in different sized areas.

3 v 3 exercise

This 3 v 3 exercise is an excellent way of giving players experience of the many situations that may occur in match play. The intensity of play and direct contact with the ball in a short space of time is invaluable.

Use an area about 12m x 12m or so with either no goals or tiny goals. Not having any goals is better in this particular situation because it's possession and passing not goal scoring, that is being practised. Physical contact is not allowed. Defenders must close down attackers and block off space but not lunge in with tackles.

There is precious little time to think about the next pass and keeping possession. This exercise can last only a few minutes because it's hard work but if played to its full potential it promotes good and quick ball control, good movement off the ball to find space and good accurate passing.

As you gain confidence the tempo should increase significantly and you start making imaginative passes into space and teammates show themselves and call well. This is where technical ability comes to the fore. Being able to make a good accurate pass to a teammate when you are under pressure makes all the ball control and kicking skills practise worthwhile.

If your team is in possession of the ball, create space if you're on the ball and find space if you're off the ball. Also, practise calling and talking to each other.

Here Katie, Aiden and Sam practise passing and moving in a 3 v 3 against Mary, Jay and Zack.

They all enjoy it and it makes them fit as well.

Mini games

Games for 4 v 4 or more need goal posts adding to create a purpose for the movement off the ball. These games encapsulate almost everything that a full size game will include but with more intensity and contact time on the ball.

New passing and moving decisions arise in competitive mini games. These decisions relate to risk and reward. In general if you are near your own goal make your passes and moves less risky to avoid your opponents getting the ball but if you are attacking the opposition goal be willing to take risks if it means being rewarded with a chance to shoot at goal.

Attacking possession

Pass and move in attack – be bold

Be prepared to make spirited penetrating, **diagonal runs** or **diagonal passes**. Perhaps disguise your pass or disguise your run depending whether you are the passer or receiver. Lose your marker by pretending to go one way then break away in the other like Wayne Rooney does on the edge of the penalty area.

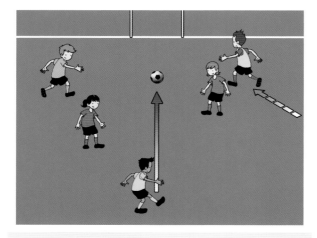

Here Zack sees a gap and makes a **diagonal run** to receive Jay's straight pass through the middle.

Zack sees Jay running straight through the line of defenders and makes a **diagonal pass** for him to run onto.

Be adventurous near the opposition goal. Make bold through ball passes because they may lead to shots at goal. If you lose possession so be it. Work to get the ball back.

Defensive Possession

Pass and move in defence – be careful.

Be careful because losing possession near your own goal can have serious consequences. Your main choices are playing the ball wide to keep possession or clearing it into touch or clearing it high up field. Clearing it into touch or high upfield probably means losing possession but it gives your team time to regroup. Alternatively you could pass through the middle if you're sure it's safe for the receiver.

Communication

You can help a teammate in possession make a good passing decision by **calling** or **signalling**.

Calling '**man on**' to a teammate receiving the ball can warn them that a defender is closing in. Calling '**time**' to the player in possession tells them they are in space and free to take the ball forward. Calling '**one – two**' can signal you want to play a wall pass past a defender because you can see space beyond the defence.

Calling the name of the player in possession can signal to them that you are in space if they need you. It may also allow the player in possession to use the caller as a 'dummy' in a dribbling move. Calling your own name can mean leave it because I'm in a strong position. The goalkeeper might call '**keepers**' to take control of the ball and situation. Zack could be about to control a pass but Oscar may call '**Oscar's**' and Zack could step over the ball leaving Oscar free in a better position.

The player in possession can call the name of the player they intend passing to so they are prepared for the pass. Emily may call '**Molly**' so Molly knows to continue her run into space and be ready for Emily's pass.

Signalling to a teammate can indicate you're available and in space. Put your **hand in the air** and a teammate may see you're in the clear and pass to you. If the player in possession is under pressure then a signal can help them make a decision quickly.

Callum has got himself into a large open space and puts his hand in the air to signal for Aiden to pass.

Aiden sees the signal and that Callum is free in an attacking position and passes the ball to him.

Perhaps **point** to the place you want the pass to go. For instance Jay, in attack, could be running along the defensive line and point for Katie, in midfield, to play the ball beyond the central defender. Katie now knows that Jay wants to run onto the ball behind the defence. He doesn't want to receive the ball to his feet.

Jay points to where he wants the ball to go and Katie duly obliges with a pass behind the defender.

They are both on the same wavelength and it leads to a penetrating attack.

Praise for good play should be used to reinforce team spirit. '**Good pass**', '**good ball**' '**good move**', '**good run**', '**good save**' to a player who has just made a good pass or created space or saved a shot is a sign of appreciation and positive motivation for the team.

Teams sometimes use calls and signals as part of their tactics. If a defence wants to push the opposition back towards their own half then a designated defender, usually a centre back, will call or signal for the defence to push up. This will leave opponents either offside or forced to retreat.

Formidable Teamwork

A team that passes and moves as a unit and works together can be formidable opposition. When you see premier league players pass and move and keep possession at pace it's awesome. That's what you should aspire to when you play.

Remember, with practise you want to become comfortable on the ball, composed under pressure, aware of the players around you and play the game with vision.

Mini games pitch

For 4 v 4 or more make the practise pitch about 30m – 40m long x 20m – 30m wide. Mark the pitch out with cones or markers. You could use existing pitch markings to help get straight lines if that's possible. Have fixed or rush (whoever is nearest the goal) goalkeepers, in goals no more than 2m wide. Play some games with the offside rule and some without it.

Oscar, Sam, Jay and Mary wear bibs so the two teams can be identified more easily.

Two sided games for six players are still feasible but they will be slower and demand more effort from each player. Make the pitch smaller and enjoy the game.

Restart the game from ball out of play

When the ball goes out of play in the mini games, restarts like throw-ins and corners can be practised.

Throw in

If the ball goes out of play over the side-line it is a throw in. Restart play with a throw in so you can practise this technique.

Aiden takes a throw in. He keeps his feet on the ground behind the side-line and throws the ball from behind his head.

Note Aiden can have his feet wide apart, with one foot in front of the other to get added distance, as long as they are both on the ground behind the touch line.

Aiden takes a quick throw and sends it in front of Molly for her to run onto.

Corners

If the defending team kicks the ball over its own goal line then it is a corner to the attacking team.

Position the ball so when you run up to kick it you don't bump into the corner flag.

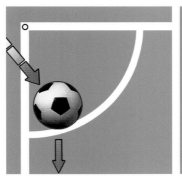 

Mary takes a corner. She could loft it for Sam to head at goal or play it on the ground to another teammate.

Left foot corner kick run up.

Right foot corner kick run up.

Goal kicks

In these small sided games a full blown goal kick would go out of play so if the attacking team kicks the ball over the defending team's dead ball line play can be restarted with the ball thrown underarm or tapped into play with your feet. Eleven-a-side goal kicks are covered in the goalkeeping section of the book.

Mini games variations

To promote and practise different aspects of football you can introduce variations to your mini games. For example to encourage using the full width of the pitch, crosses and changes of direction, play four goal games.

Another alternative would be to stipulate that each team must have at least one player in each half of the pitch at all times. This would encourage open play and the use of pass backs to keep possession and change the direction of the attack. Another variation would be mini games with no-go zones or limited access zones in the attacking third, which would also promote wide play and movement off the ball.

Four goal game

To promote use of the wings (the space near the touchlines) and challenge thought processes widen the pitch and shorten it and add a second set of goals for each team to attack and defend. Make the pitch about 25m long x 30m wide with goals about 1.2m wide near each corner.

Callum is attacking the goal being defended by Molly and Oscar when he sees Aiden making a run towards the undefended goal so Callum turns and sends a fine pass for Aiden to run onto and threaten the second goal.

Keep your head up and you should soon get the hang of seeing gaps towards the far goal as defenders get sucked in to protect the attacked goal.

SHOOTING AND ATTACKING

Scoring goals is fundamental to success in competitive football matches, so shooting and attacking are major skills to learn. At its simplest, a shot is a pass to the net but it doesn't have to be weighted like a pass. As long as the shot is on target and crosses the line it can be driven or tapped into the net. Keeping the shot on target is the major challenge.

Shooting situations

Each attacking situation is unique and you must be prepared to adapt to take any chance of shooting at goal. Sometimes you may be off balance or stretching but must still try to control the shot. Here are some examples of shooting situations.

Sam's driven shot from inside the penalty area gives the goalkeeper no chance.

Emily sees the goalkeeper off the line and chips the ball over his head.

Here the goalkeeper has advanced to narrow the angle but Sam quickly touches the ball left and side foots it into the far corner of the net.

The goalkeeper advances and dives to block a drive but instead, Jay chips the ball over the goalkeepers spread-eagled body.

Oscar gambles on a pass to the near post and runs onto a brilliant cross to side foot volley the ball into the corner of the net.

The goalkeeper makes a good block but can only parry the shot out and the alert Emily runs in to score an easy goal.

Types of shot

There are as many types of shot as there are types of kick. The usual shots are drive, side foot, volley, half volley, chip and lob. The ball may be dribbled round the goalkeeper or passed into the net. If you're technically gifted you can even deliberately bend the ball past the goalkeeper.

Driven shots

The driven shot is the most powerful of all shots. It is not the most accurate but if struck well and on target is difficult to stop.

As with all shots on goal, use your eyes to notice where the goal and goalkeeper are. In the instant you decide what shot to make, concentrate on the ball. Base your driven shot shooting technique on the low drive kick shown earlier in the book. Try to point your toes down and get your knee over, or in line with, the ball to execute the shot.

Many driven shots, even at the highest level, miss the goal because players lean back or point their toes up too soon on the follow through and the ball rises wildly over the cross bar. Players like Steven Gerrard have a good success rate with driven shots because they apply the correct technique during the game.

Increasing power

Lack of power is a common issue for beginners. Lack of power isn't necessarily about lack of physical size or strength, it may be about the "sweetness" of the foot's contact with the ball. "Sweetness" is related to how the body shapes up to address the ball and the quality and timing of the contact with the ball.

The top of the foot is a small area of the foot to hit the ball with and if contact is made with the foot slightly off centre then all power and direction are lost. It is a very fine line between a successful drive and a miscued drive. The more you practise the better your contact and timing becomes and you will hit the ball sweeter, generating more power in the shot.

Wall drives

You can successfully practise alone to increase power by shooting against a wall. You get a lot of kicks in a short time and it improves power and accuracy.

Ryan pushes the ball forward and steps up to it ready to drive the ball. He starts by driving it gently with one foot to get his stance and contact point on the ball established.

Gradually Ryan's increasing the power as he gets better, and now the ball fizzes at the wall because his timing and contact are sweet.

Repeat the exercise with the other foot so your driven shots with either foot improve.

Roll out drives

Get the coach, or a friend, to roll the ball out from goal to you and then touch it forward before hitting it when it stops or as it's still rolling. Kicking a ball moving away slowly helps coordinate the shot.

 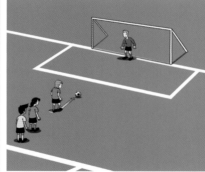 

Here the coach rolls the ball out to each player in turn. Molly starts and is ready to receive the ball just beyond the penalty spot.

When the ball reaches her she cushions it forward and after a glance at the goal …

… steps up and drives the ball into the bottom right hand corner of the net.

That's the way, Molly.

It feels good to strike a drive sweetly. You'll know if you hit a drive well, because it will rocket to its destination with what seems like little effort on your part.

Volley, half volley and lob shots

Hitting a volley shot on goal can be very difficult. You may have time to think about it as it flies in from the wing or it may suddenly appear from a ruck of players inside the penalty area. Either way, keeping the shot down and on target are the main priorities.

Volley off cones practise

To get used to hitting volleys, start with a static ball held in the air by a cone. Take it in turns to volley balls set up on different height cones. Shape up for the shot with your body nearly horizontal.

Jay is shaping up horizontally and getting his foot over the ball to keep it down.

Volley from short bounced ball practise

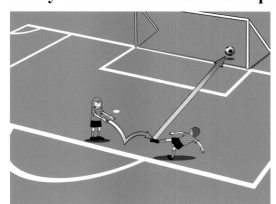

Progress to practise in pairs with a moving ball. Take it in turns for one player to bounce the ball for the other player to volley. Adjust your standing foot to suit the flight of the ball.

Practise from the left and right.

Here Sam hits a sweet left foot volley from Molly's bounced ball.

Volley from ball bouncing back off wall practise

Sam is throwing the ball at the wall so it bounces back. Sam then moves his feet into position, shapes up with his body nearly horizontal and kicks the ball while it's in the air back against the wall. This exercise can be repeated many times in a few minutes to improve volleying ability. Aim the volley at different parts of the wall to develop control and accuracy. Try it with both feet from the front and side.

Sam demonstrates a volley shot

Sam sees a cross from the left and runs into space to meet it. He hits a powerful left-footed volley from a well balanced stance. He knows where the goal is and his eyes are now focused directly on the ball.

Practise has made Sam good at volleying.

Half volley

Gently pop the ball up in the air in front of you and let it drop at your feet. Strike the ball as it touches the ground. Timing is crucial for a good kick.

As with most half volleys, Oscar is standing upright.

Joe Cole scored a difficult half volley goal against Estonia in 2007 when, with his back to goal, he chested a high ball to the ground, then turned and fired a half volley into the net. There were several difficult techniques combined together to score that goal.

Lob

Lobbed shots can clear defenders in a crowded penalty area or they can result when an attacker is quick to respond to a bouncing through pass over the defence.

Here the goalkeeper comes out to try and parry a shot but Jay lobs the bouncing ball with his side foot over the goalkeeper's head into the net.

Your side foot will be more accurate but the top of your foot will get more distance.

Increase your chance of scoring

Be accurate

When you are about to shoot keep your eye on the ball and be quick but in control. Relax and try not to snatch the shot. Timing and good contact with the ball should lead to an accurate, well placed shot on target.

Be on the move and aware

If you anticipate, or gamble, where the ball is going to go and move towards it you will be far harder to mark than an attacker standing still. This will create space and time for your control and shot.

Make it hard for the goalkeeper

Keep your shot low because it is further for a goalkeeper to get down to a low shot. Perhaps disguise your intentions and feint to shoot and as the goalkeeper goes to ground dribble past or chip the ball over the goalkeeper into the net.

Consider striking the ball across the goalkeeper into the far corner of the net. There are several reasons for this. One is that if you are approaching from off centre the goalkeeper will move across to narrow the angle and protect the near post so it will be more difficult for the goalkeeper to change direction and dive on the ball. Another reason to shoot to the far post is that a teammate may be able to run onto the ball or pounce on a goalkeeper parry to strike the ball into the net.

Katie runs in on goal and as the goalkeeper comes out she hits the ball left-footed low across goal into the far corner. The goalkeeper has no chance to get down to the shot.

That was a good accurate shot close to the goalkeeper's feet, Katie.

Be a predator

Be a predator in front of goal. Look for opportunities from rebounds, miss-kicks, fumbles or ricochets and pounce on defensive errors. Follow up teammates' shots in case the goalkeeper parries them out towards you. Top goal scorers at any level of football get many goals from goalmouth scrambles and tap in goals from very close in. Gary Lineker used to poach many goals from inside the six yard box.

Aiden follows up Sam's shot just in case he doesn't score.

Sam's shot beats the goalkeeper but hits the post and rebounds across goal.

Aiden is left with a simple tap in after putting in the effort to follow the shot up.

Shooting and attacking exercises

Shooting on goal is good fun and there are many practise routines to keep players stimulated. After players have shot at goal they must always collect the ball and return it to the queue so there are enough balls available for everyone else.

Freestyle shooting

A simple exercise to build kicking strength and distance judgement is to take turns at shooting on goal from the edge of the penalty area.

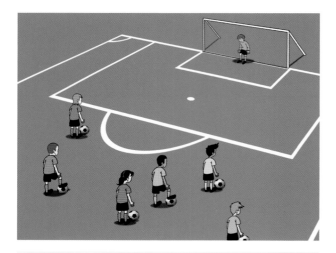

Molly's turn is next and she drives the ball hard at goal …

… high into the top left corner of the goal easily beating the goalkeeper. Molly, that's your best goal so far.

Dribble and shoot exercise

In a match you may receive the ball just outside the penalty area and dribble forward before taking a shot. To prepare for this happening line up at one cone and take turns to dribble left or right of an obstacle and have a shot at goal. Shots are taken both left and right-footed with any type of kick.

If you score, congratulations.

Here Ryan, the first attacker, dribbles to the right of the cone and shoots on goal from just inside the penalty area. Tom practises shot saving.

Ryan drives his shot low and hard across goal and beats the keeper at the far post.

A classic goal, Ryan.

Here Jay goes left of the cone and pushes the ball too far but as Tom comes out to dive at his feet Jay chips the ball left-footed over him into the net.

That was cool, Jay.

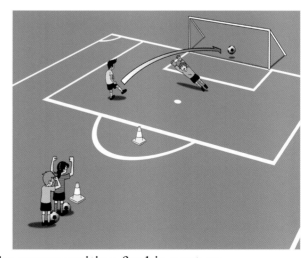

Jay collects his ball and joins the back of the queue waiting for his next go.

One-two and shoot exercise

During a match, to divert the defenders' attention away from your movement you may play a one-two with a teammate, who has their back to goal, to create space for a shot at goal.

Line up at one cone and take turns to play a one-two with a teammate either to the left or right of the 'D' at the edge of the penalty area, control the ball and have a shot at goal. Shots are taken both left and right-footed with any type of kick.

Ryan stands in the D with the other players lined up at the cone. Jay passes the ball to Ryan and sets off running to receive the return pass.

Ryan lays the ball off, first touch, to Jay.

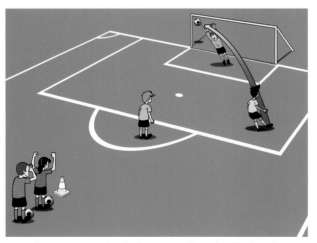

Jay touches the ball forward and decides to float the ball high into the top corner over the goalkeeper's head.

That was accurate, Jay.

Remember to control the moving ball, look up to see where you are going to place the shot and then focus on the ball to make good contact for a successful shot on target.

Over the shoulder shooting exercise

Sometimes the ball is hit over the defence and you have to run on to it, control it and shoot. This exercise emulates a high through ball pass, control and shot.

Take turns to have the ball thrown over your head for you to turn, control the ball and have a shot at goal. Shots are taken both left and right-footed with any type of kick.

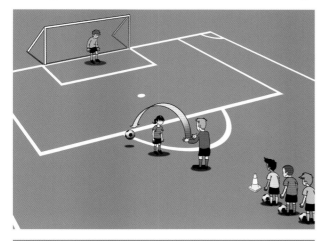

Katie faces the coach who throws the ball over her shoulder.

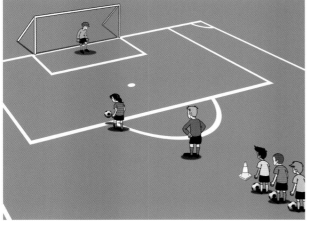

Katie turns, looks to see where she is going to place the shot, adjusts her position relative to the bouncing ball and as it comes down she focuses and…

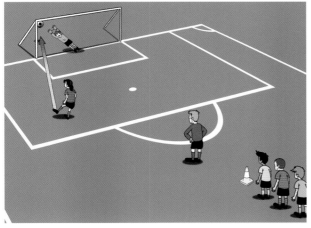

… with her eyes on the ball Katie volleys the ball left-footed into the top left corner of the goal.

That was an unstoppable shot, Katie.

To improve your chances of striking a successful volley you need to 1. Be mobile and get your body and feet in position. 2. Strike the ball when it's on the way down. 3. Hit the ball sweetly and accurately rather than with power. A sweetly struck volley will fly into the net.

After ten shots each from the left repeat the exercise from the right, shooting with your right foot.

Cut inside and shoot exercise

Opportunities to shoot sometimes come when you cut inside from the wing. You may dribble infield from the left wing and shoot at goal with your right foot, or dribble in field from the right wing and shoot at goal with your left foot.

Create a small slalom course with poles to dribble through and a gate at the beginning so that you emerge from the last pole away from the goal then shoot at goal.

Callum sets off through the gate and dribbles through the obstacle course as if he were cutting across defenders.

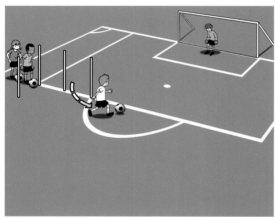

When Callum rounds the last pole he sets himself up …

… and fires a thunderbolt drive into the net.

That's impressive, Callum.

This is a tricky shot because you have to almost wrap your foot round the ball to make it change direction dramatically.

Callum collects his ball and joins the back of the queue. After ten shots each from the left repeat the exercise from the right, shooting with your left foot.

Attacking in pairs

Many opportunities to create goals come from near the touch line wide on the wing or at narrow angles close into the goal. The player wide, or at a narrow angle, has only a remote chance of scoring directly but if the player passes to a teammate in the middle, square on the goal, a good goal scoring opportunity may be created.

Wide attack

Cross to centre from wing and shoot exercise

One set of players on the wing with a ball each take turns to dribble round a cone and cross to a player waiting to control the cross and shoot at goal. The player receiving the ball should delay their run so they are still moving forward when the ball arrives. This gives defenders a minimum amount of time to get close.

With Tom in goal Emily dribbles down the wing and crosses a lofted ball left-footed into the penalty area where Sam runs onto the ball.

Depending how the ball arrives Sam could either hit it first time or take a touch to control it.

Sam decides to cushion the ball right-footed onto his left to volley into the net.

Classy control and good finishing, Sam.

Keep your head up and be aware of the position of the goal, the goalkeeper and the ball as it is crossed. When the ball gets close, focus on it for good control and shooting.

Emily joins the back of the shooting queue and Sam collects the ball and joins the back of the crossing queue. This way each player takes turns crossing and shooting. Keep the routine moving until you've all had ten or so crosses from the left. Repeat the exercise from the right wing.

Narrow angle attack

It is difficult to score a goal directly from near the dead ball line because of the narrow angle. The goalkeeper is likely to be protecting the near goal post too. A goal from a direct narrow angle shot is spectacular and rare, but it is always tempting to shoot from such close range and not play the simple ball. The simple ball is the pass to a teammate in the middle who is more likely to score a goal than a direct shot from the narrow angle.

Narrow angle pass and shoot exercise

One set of players line up with footballs ready to dribble to the dead ball line while the second group are standing at a cone outside the penalty area. Working in pairs one player should dribble to the cone and pass and the other receives the ball and either hits first time with control, or cushions the ball forward with one foot for the other foot to strike. In this exercise the first touch and strike depends on how the ball arrives and the goalkeeper's position.

With the cones set up on the right side of goal inside the penalty area near the goal line Sam takes his turn to dribble and pass while Mary waits to receive the pass and shoot.

With Tom or the coach in goal Sam dribbles the ball round the cone and side foots the ball to Mary who times her run to meet the ball at the edge of the penalty area.

Mary cushions the ball forward with her left side foot and drives the ball low into the bottom right corner with his right foot.

That was clinical, Mary.

Mary collects the ball and joins the back of the passing group and Sam joins the back of the shooting group. Repeat the exercise ten times or so from both sides of the goal.

Put a cone on the penalty spot to act as a defender for more experienced players to get past.

Where's the goalkeeper during all this shooting practise?

Goalkeepers get excellent practise when others are shooting at goal. They should have free rein to defend the shots as they see fit. It gives them the opportunity to practise saving from different players who use different techniques and styles.

However, the goalkeeper must not be bombarded with hard shots from close in for too long. To maintain interest and avoid overworking, the coach should let the regular goalkeeper come out of goal and join in the shooting practise. Another player could volunteer or the coach could go in goal for a while.

If goalkeeper joins in the shooting practise it will increase their understanding of the attacking game, which can only help when it comes to making saves. It will also enhance their ball skills and give them more confidence to deal with pass backs and goal kicks.

Free kicks and penalties

Free kicks direct at goal and penalties are shots with a static ball not in open play.

Free kicks

Without a defending wall free kick practise is not particularly realistic but it's not much fun being a defender in a wall whilst others have pot shots at goal.

Practise free kicks taking it in turns to be in the wall. Half the players form the wall and the other players take a couple of turns each taking a free kick directly at goal.

Here Jay lines up to shoot the ball over the wall into the top right corner of the net.

Jay clears the wall and shoots on target but it's straight at Tom and he clutches the ball to his chest.

With the wall players now shooting Molly lofts the ball into the right corner of the goal.

Good goal, Molly.

One way of practising free kicks and avoiding players being hurt in the wall is to use imitation defenders. Buy imitation players from sports shops or make your own. Perhaps use a row of exercise poles or corner flags. This will allow more free kicks to be practised safely.

Penalties

If an attacking player is fouled inside the opposition penalty area a penalty is awarded to the attacking team. The penalty is taken with the ball placed on the penalty spot twelve yards from the goal. Only the goalkeeper and penalty taker are allowed inside the penalty box before the penalty kick is taken.

Penalty shoot-out exercise

Penalties are occasionally given in competitive matches and it is worthwhile practising penalties in preparation for the drama of the real thing.

One way to make penalty practise interesting is to introduce competition with a penalty shoot out. Each player should take a penalty in turn until only one successful player is left. Players can't be out first round so each player gets to take at least two penalties. The rule is you stand out if you miss or the penalty is saved. The goalkeeper should take a turn as well, with someone else going in goal.

This practise allows each player to find out what sort of penalty they like taking.

It's also good for confidence because taking a penalty is an exposed and solitary activity. Getting used to taking penalties with other players watching is good experience.

Oscar puts the ball on the spot to take the first penalty.

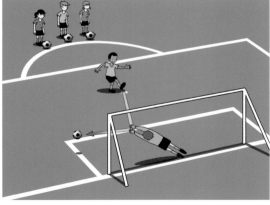

And chips it to Tom's left but Tom makes a brilliant save.

Oscar's lucky because he can't be out first round.

He'll get a second chance.

One penalty shoot-out alternative is to take 5 penalties each, say, and keep a record of the penalties scored. The player with the highest score wins. Have a sudden death shoot out if more than one player is level top scorer.

Another alternative is to arrange yourselves into two teams and have a team penalty shoot-out competition like in the World Cup.

Offside

If you're in your opponent's half when the ball is kicked forward to you and there is only one player between you and the goal you are **offside**. The offside law enables the defenders to force the attackers back to their own half and prevents them just waiting for a long pass or "goal hanging". See page 145 for more details about the offside rule.

It can take a few seasons for young enthusiastic players to discipline themselves enough to stay on side and run onto the ball only after it has been passed to them.

To avoid promising attacks breaking down in offside frustration a little practise to understand how to stay on side will help.

Stay on side exercise

To promote staying on side to beat the offside trap set up a row of cones as defenders and get each player to pass the ball to the coach and run to the line of defenders. The coach deliberately delays the pass so the player stops before running onto the ball when it is passed.

Katie passes to the coach and runs to the defensive line and looks along it both ways to make sure she is on side.

The coach delays the pass until Katie is forced to stand onside.

The coach passes the ball beyond the defenders and Katie, on side when the ball was passed, immediately sets off to catch it.

This simple exercise gets you thinking about your position relative to defenders before the ball is played.

Beat the offside trap at pace

To improve your chance of getting to the ball before a defender, run, on side, along the line of defenders until the pass is made and then quickly change direction running successfully behind the defenders onto the pass.

Run along the line and break clear exercise

Half the players line up with footballs while the other half are out wide, ready to run.

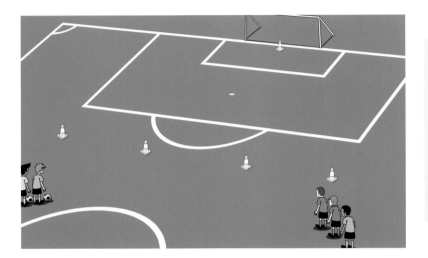

Sam runs across the defenders making sure he stays on side.

Ryan waits until Sam is clear of one defender and passes the ball behind another.

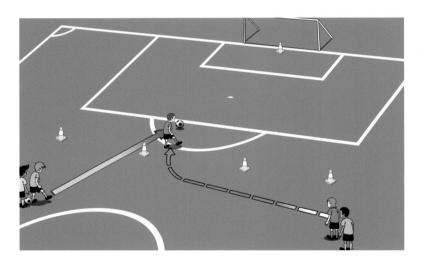

Sam sees the pass released and quickly changes direction to break beyond the defence onto the ball and have a shot at goal.

Sam takes the ball to the back of the passing queue and Ryan joins the back of the attackers' queue.

It's worth noting you can't be offside from a goal kick, corner or throw in, so get beyond the opposition and take advantage of these rules if the opportunity arises.

You also cannot be offside if you're behind the attacker in possession of the ball, so follow their attack ready to receive a pass.

DRIBBLING AND RUNNING WITH THE BALL

Dribbling and running with the ball is fun. A player who is comfortable on the ball is a major asset to the team, so the ability to dribble should be encouraged. Dribbling and running with the ball are close control on the move. They are the most individual of outfield activities, but there are still some techniques you can learn which can form the basis of your own dribbling skills.

Dribbling Skills

Dribbling is the art of taking the ball past opponents and should be encouraged in all young players. This applies to defenders as well as attackers. Dribbling is an attacking skill, which is risky to employ in defensive positions but it is important that defenders are skilful at dribbling to increase their confidence on the ball and increase the attacking options available to a team. It is a skill all players should learn.

Contact zone

Contact can be made with many parts of the foot when dribbling so in this section we'll talk about the inside, outside, top, toes, sole and heel of each foot. The contact zone on the ball can be any part of it.

Your touch on the ball should be confident and gentle.

Keep the ball close when dribbling.

Dribbling needs a high level of ball control and the most comfortable and sensitive control is achieved using the forward part of the inside or outside of each foot near your toes. Do not use your toe end because it is too hard and insensitive (gives no feel). The sole of the foot is also sometimes used to roll the ball.

Pace, feints, change of direction and tricks

The dribbling techniques used to get past opponents fall into four main categories. They are all useful in different circumstances. You may use change of **pace** to push the ball past the defender and accelerate away explosively or to slow them up before you accelerate away. You could use a **feint** where you pretend to go one way to wrong foot the defender and then take the ball the other way. A sudden **change of direction** can leave a defender off balance and beaten. You could sometimes use **tricks** where you do something unusual and surprise your opponent, like the double drag back Maradona perfected.

Pace

Just as the name suggests if you can see the space beyond the defender and feel confident push the ball past the defender and explode beyond them. Change of pace is also effective. If the defender is running alongside you, as Paul Gascoigne used to do, you could slow down to slow the defender, then set off quickly again leaving the defender trailing.

Feints

A good feint can either **convince** or **confuse** a defender. A well executed feint can make the defender certain they know where you're going and that you're setting off now. To convince them use your entire body. Drop your shoulder, rotate your hips, prepare to push off your standing foot and 'skin' the ball with your kicking foot. 'Skin' the ball means get your kicking foot so close to the ball when you are pretending to kick it that you may even touch it. Once you've deceived the defender into committing themselves to go one way waste no time in going the other way and getting beyond them.

Multiple feints may confuse a defender so much that they haven't got a clue which way you're going.

An exaggerated feint to shoot, or pass, will get a reaction from a defender giving you time to push and go into space. But feints do not have to be outrageous to be successful. They can be subtle but they must be convincing. Waggling your kicking foot nowhere near the ball will convince no one, but a subtle shimmy with you hips and slight drop of the shoulder may wrong foot the defender completely.

Jay drops his left shoulder, swivels his hip and 'skins' the ball with his right foot as if, for all the world, he is going left.

Which way is Jay going?

This way?

No this way.

He's just convinced the defender into thinking he's going left but Jay is taking the ball to the right.

Change of direction

To change direction suddenly and leave a defender behind needs very close ball control and superb balance. You must be able to play the ball with equal ease with the inside and outside of both feet. Defenders will feel very uncomfortable if they know you can change direction at will. Pelé and George Best in the past were both masters of this skill as is Ryan Giggs today.

Tricks

Tricks confuse defenders with the unexpected. Examples of tricks when dribbling are the Maradona double drag back and Ronaldinho's drag back and play the ball behind his other leg. Perhaps the most commonly used tricks are the back heel and the nutmeg where the ball is played between an opponents' legs.

Double drag back

Oscar is dribbling the ball straight at an opponent and when he reaches them he puts the sole of his left foot on the ball and rolls or drags it back.

As he drags it back, Oscar spins in the air clockwise, turning his back to the defender and switches feet so his right foot is now on top of the ball. With his right foot he drags the ball back again and continues his spin …

… clockwise until he is facing forwards again. Oscar now continues his run, with the ball at his feet, beyond the bemused defender.

That was amazing, Oscar! Do it again, I can't believe it.

Nutmeg

Callum is running down the wing with the ball at his feet when a defender comes quickly across to block his progress.

As the defender's foot comes out to block the ball, Callum nutmegs the defender and cuts inside to carry on the attack leaving the defender stranded.

Clever trick Callum. Your timing was excellent.

Drag back and play the ball behind you

If you are caught in a tight situation then using the sole of your foot to roll or drag the ball backwards or sideways can be a useful trick to create space.

Emily has the ball in midfield when an opponent comes running across to block her run. Quickly she puts her right foot on top of the ball and drags it back behind her left foot …

… and then plays the ball with her right side foot left behind her left leg in the direction the defender has just come from.

Good control, Emily. You completely fooled the defender with that trick.

Ronaldinho does this trick quite often but it always works because the defender cannot reach the ball.

Develop touch, control and awareness

Be comfortable with the ball at your feet

Become a master craftsman of ball control. Practise touching and moving the ball with different parts of your feet. Touch it left and right with the inside and outside of each foot. Roll it sideways left and right with the sole of each foot. Roll it forwards and backwards with the sole of each foot. Move it forwards and backwards with the inside and outside of each foot.

Emily and Sam practise freestyle dribbling ball control.

Here, Emily is dragging the ball back several paces with the sole of her foot and Sam is moving the ball right with the outside of his right foot.

As your touch and control skill levels improve, introduce an imaginary opponent into the practise. Sprint away with a sudden surge of pace for a few strides, or feint to touch the ball one way and go the other or confuse the imaginary opponent with a drag back trick.

Move the ball from foot to foot

Balance and co-ordination are important when dribbling. Playing the ball from one foot to the other tests this ability with the constant shifting of balance from left to right.

Start with simply playing the ball sideways left and right between your feet. Touch the ball with the forward inside of each foot. The ball must roll and you must stay on your toes keeping well balanced and comfortable. Develop the skill so you don't have to look directly at the ball. The ideal is to keep your head up to see around you and keep the ball in your peripheral vision but still under control.

Increase the speed that the ball moves to and fro as you get better.

As you get more confident develop this important skill further by moving forwards or backwards while still playing the ball side to side from one foot to the other.

Dribbling awareness exercise

Learning dribbling ball skills solo is important. The next stage is to use those skills in an unpredictable environment. Assemble with a football each in an area the size of the centre circle and dribble randomly with the ball in and around other players and obstacles. Keep your head up so you don't bump into other players but can see the ball and keep it under control. Touch the ball often and change direction a lot too. Play the ball with the front inside and outside of the foot for maximum control and also touch the ball with different parts of each foot including the sole to see how it feels. You will gradually find your favourite method of touching and moving the ball in a crowd.

Close control exercise

A simple dribble is to run at the defender with the ball, touch it to the side with one foot, then push it forward with the other foot beyond the defender and run after it. Two players can practise this quickfire touch-touch technique facing each other, no further than 1m apart. Pass the ball clockwise from your left foot to your right foot then to your partner's left foot and so on. Get on your toes and be well balanced. Try to get a rhythm going.

Jay starts with the ball at his left foot and touches it to his right foot and with one touch passes the ball to Oscar.

Oscar controls and moves the ball from his left foot to his right foot in one movement and immediately passes it to Jay's left foot.

Continue clockwise for 30 seconds and then change to go anti-clockwise.

Slalom dribble exercise

A traditional, but effective, method of dribbling practise is to place cones at about 3m centres and take turns dribbling in and out of them.

Here Katie is dribbling round the cones keeping the ball under close control.

She'll pass the ball to Ryan when she gets past the last cone and join the back of the queue.

Ryan's moving quickly through the obstacles using the inside of his left foot to pass a cone on the left and the inside of his right foot to pass a cone on the right.

The spacing of the cones can be varied to suit the exercise. If they are close together, then the routine is more akin to dribbling and if further apart the routine is more like running with the ball. Vary the routine to use the right or left foot only or both feet.

Hone your dribbling skills

The effective application of dribbling techniques comes with practise and experience. Find out which techniques work for you and practise them until you can apply them successfully. Always have several types of dribble that you can do and be prepared to pass the defender on the left or right so you don't become predictable. It's always good to have an armoury of tricks and skills. Cristiano Ronaldo has a vast array of dribbling skills using pace, feints, change of direction and tricks, which is why he's such a successful dribbler.

Control the situation

When you have the ball and you're trying to dribble past a defender make sure you control the situation. Be proactive and keep the ball moving and keep it close, don't let the defender seize the initiative and dummy you into touching the ball into open space. This is when your close control and dribbling skills come to the fore. Keep the defender guessing and sow doubt in their mind.

Your early dribbling attempts may be foiled but keep going and your feints will get more subtle, your movement will become slick and fast, your tricks will surprise them and your change of pace will leave them in your wake.

Shield the ball

A particular case, which occurs often is where you receive the ball with your back to goal and a defender closes you down so quickly you can't turn to attack them. If you're in possession and caught with your back to goal be prepared to shield the ball by getting your body between the ball and the defender.

Here Oscar has his back to goal with a defender pressing very close. Oscar has his arms out to prevent the defender getting round him easily.

It is legal to hold your arms out wide to prevent an opponent getting round you but don't grab hold of them or push them because that is a foul.

If the defender is jockeying from the side, shield the ball again by getting your body between the defender and the ball.

Successful dribbling techniques

There are many dribbling styles used by professional footballers. Watch them at matches or on TV and copy the ones you like or develop your own unique dribble and surprise defenders.

As dribbling is such an individual skill we'll let the players demonstrate their own favourite dribbling technique to you. Each dribble should be practised left and right-footed.

The team are going to show you twelve different dribbles and if you mastered them all you would terrify defenders.

You go first, Mary

This is a dribble based on the passing between feet exercises shown earlier on. It's particularly effective if the defender is square on and either static or rushing towards you. It is based on pace and is achievable without breaking your stride. Mary's dribble looks like this from the side.

Mary is moving the ball forward using her left inside foot with each stride.	As the defender steps forward to tackle her she touches the ball across her body from her left foot to her right foot without feinting …	… and immediately touches the ball forward with the inside of her right foot as she strides forward. The ball and Mary move rapidly past the defender leaving them stranded.

From above the touches on the ball are as follows

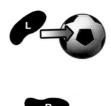 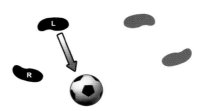 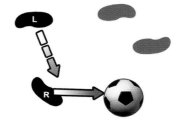

Touch ball forward.	Mary plays the ball across her body.	Then she plays it forward beyond the defender and continues her run.

From the front Mary's dribble looks like this

Mary moving the ball forward.	Mary plays the ball across her body and across the defender.	Then instantly plays the ball forward and past the defender.

Well done, Mary. You quickly left the defender behind with that fast footwork technique.

What's your dribble, Oscar?

This is one of the dribbles that uses a feint and explosive pace to get past the defender. It was made famous a long time ago by Sir Stanley Matthews and is still used today to great effect. From the side Oscar's actions look like this.

Oscar is moving the ball down the wing using alternate right outside and right inside foot touches to move the ball forward.

Oscar feints to play the ball with a right inside foot touch towards the left to deceive and off balance the defender …

… but instantly moves his right foot behind the ball and plays it right outside-footed past the defender.

From above the touches on the ball and feints are as follows

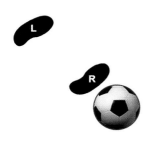

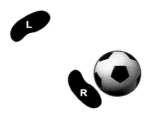

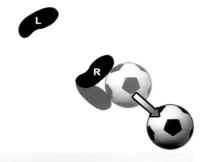

Dribble the ball forward.

Feint to go left.

Move foot to other side of ball and go right.

From the front you can see Oscar's shoulder drop to go left and the explosive push off his left foot to take the ball right and past the defender.

Oscar drops his left shoulder and puts his right foot to the ball and feints as if to go left.

But quickly moves his right foot to the other side of the ball and plays it right.

Oscar pushes off hard from his left foot to accelerate away from the defender.

Show us your favourite dribble, Katie

Katie's is a change of pace stop-start dribble. This dribble stops or slows the opponent up when they are running alongside you so you can accelerate away. Paul Gascoigne used this type of manoeuvre before accelerating away from opponents. From the side Katie plays the ball like this.

Katie is running with the ball at her feet and the defender is close beside her on the left threatening to make a tackle or block the run …

… so Katie half turns and feints to play the ball back in the direction she has come from and the defender turns to intercept the move.

But Katie doesn't play the ball back and returns to carry on her run leaving the defender behind and gaining extra yards to get clear.

Good feint and change of pace, Katie.

From above the feint and touches on the ball are as follows

 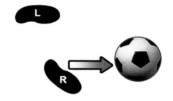

Katie playing the ball forward.

Katie feints to go back so the defender turns or stops.

Katie continues her run but now with yards of space.

From the front Katie's stop start dribble looks like this

Katie dribbling the ball forward.

Katie feinting to slow the defender.

Katie continues on her forward run accelerating away from the defender.

Your turn, Sam

This dribble makes the defender think you are going to pass out wide but you drag the ball back across the front of your body and go the other way. Michael Owen sometimes does this on the edge of the penalty area. From the side Sam's movement looks like this.

Sam is confronted by a defender in front of goal so he shapes up to pass the ball out wide to a teammate but sees the defender anticipate and move across early to intercept the imagined pass.

So Sam, without making the pass, puts his foot around the far side of the ball and hooks it back across the front of his body.

Sam pushes off hard in the other direction creating space for a shot on goal and leaving the defender completely out of position.

From above the touches on the ball are as follows

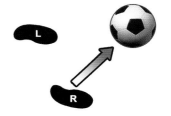

Feint to pass the ball wide.

Hook your foot round the ball.

... and fetch it across your body to create space.

From the front Sam's feinted pass dribble looks like this

Sam convinces the defender he's about to pass out wide right.

But no he isn't. Sam hooks his foot round the ball and drags it across his body …

… and goes left to strike left-footed on goal.

You created that space from nothing, Sam.

Here's a double feint by Aiden

In this dribble Aiden confuses the defender by feinting to go left then right then really moves left in the original feinted direction. The defender's totally confused by this stage. Cristiano Ronaldo uses this dribble to devastating effect. From the side Aiden's feint goes like this.

Aiden feints right-footed to go left but moves his right foot behind and to the other side of the ball.	Aiden changes his body balance again, drops his right shoulder and to all intents and purposes appears to be playing the ball with the outside of his right foot to the right of the defender.	But no, Aiden lifts his right foot over the top of the ball and goes left in the direction of the original feint. Aiden has performed an excellent double feint.

From above the foot movements on the ball are as follows

Skin the ball and feint to go left.	Move round ball and step over feint to go right.	Go left.

From the front Aiden's pronounced step over feint can be seen clearly

Aiden feints to go left and moves his foot round to the other side of the ball.	Aiden feints to go right stepping over the ball.	Then bursts away to the left leaving the defender confused.

Molly, what's your dribble?

Molly's dribble is useful if you are caught with your back to goal with a defender closing you down. You can feint to go one way then go the other to create space to turn leaving the defender chasing shadows. From the side Molly feints and turns like this.

Molly receives the ball to her feet with a defender tight behind her. She cannot turn so …	… she feints to go left across the defender. Molly drops her left shoulder and pretends to touch the ball wide left with her right foot but at the last moment …	Molly brings her right foot across and behind the ball and plays it right. She pushes hard off her left foot to get clear of the defender.

From above the approach is as follows

  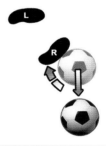

Molly receives the ball.	Molly feints to go left.	Molly moves her foot to the left and goes right.

From the front Molly shrugs the defender off like this

Molly receives the pass and with her arms out to shield the ball …	… she feints as if to go left.	But moves her foot to the other side of the ball and explodes away in the other direction.

Ryan's dribble

This dribble is a change of direction-cum-nutmeg manoeuvre. If defenders are running beside you and you can read their stride pattern you can play the ball sideways between their legs just before their leading leg touches the ground. Pelé turned defenders inside out with similar moves. Kaka does the same today. From the side Ryan performs this difficult close control dribble like this.

Ryan is dribbling the ball forward with a persistent defender on his right shadowing him.	The defender is striding out assuming Ryan will continue along the same line but Ryan notices the long strides and …	… plays the ball between the defender's legs and cuts across behind him to advance on the goal.

From above the touches on the ball are as follows

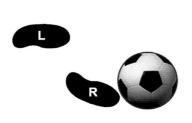 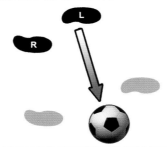 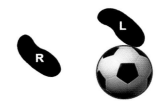

Dribble the ball forward.	Play the ball between the defender's legs.	Change direction and dribble away from the defender.

From the front

Ryan dribbles the ball forward with the defender close beside him.	Ryan plays the ball sideways between the defender's legs and ….	…. quickly changes direction to run into open space.

The change of direction can also be performed across the front or behind the defender and you could change direction many times to baffle the defender before you finally make your move.

Jay's dribble

This dribble is a single step over and play the ball with the other foot like Cristiano Ronaldo. From the side Jay's speedy moves beat the defender like this.

Jay is moving quickly playing the ball forward with the outside of his right foot …

… and then moves his whole body right and steps over the ball right-footed as if to go right.

But, using his natural stride pattern, immediately redirects the ball left with the outside of his left foot so he can go past the off balance defender at speed.

From above the touches on the ball are as follows

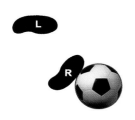 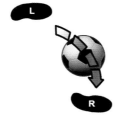 

Play the ball forward right-footed.

Move whole body right and step over the ball with your right foot.

Play the ball left and go beyond the defender.

From the front Jay's rapid movement can be seen clearly.

Jay is running forward towards the defender.

Jay feints to go right and steps over the ball moving his whole body right.

Jay goes left.

Well done, Jay. That was a blur of speed.

Emily, it's your turn to show us your favourite dribble now

This dribble, made famous by Johann Cruyff, creates space to cross the ball from the wing. From the side Emily's feint does the job.

Emily is running with the ball down the left wing with a defender running alongside. Emily feints to cross left-footed …

… to force the defensive block tackle but instead wraps her left foot round the ball and plays it behind her other leg …

… quickly turns and crosses the ball right-footed.

From above the touches on the ball are as follows

 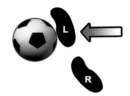 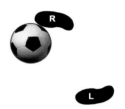

Feint to cross left-footed.

Wrap left foot around the ball and touch it back.

Turn and cross in space with the other foot.

From the front Emily's feint and turn can be clearly seen

Feint to cross left-footed.

Drag the ball behind right foot with left foot.

Turn and cross right-footed.

Well done, Emily. That's a great method of beating a good defender from either wing. It helps that you're two-footed.

Callum's dribble

This dribble is a feint to convince the defender you're going to control the moving ball but you let it run across your body and move quickly away beyond the defender. From the side Callum fools the defender like this.

Callum sees the ball approaching him from the left and feints as if to control the ball but instead …

… pulls his right foot away and lets the ball run across the front of his body.

Callum turns and runs with the ball clear of the flat-footed defender.

From above the feet movements and feint on the ball are as follows

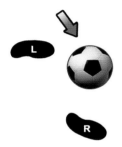

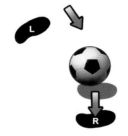

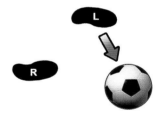

Ball approaches from the left.

Feint to pass or control the ball with right foot.

Let the ball run on beyond the defender.

From the front Callum's simple ruse has been effective

Callum pretends to control the ball …

… but withdraws his right foot at the last moment and lets the ball run by.

Callum quickly turns to run forward with the ball at his feet.

Zack's dribble

This dribble is a double step over as perfected by Ryan Giggs. You need to be well balanced and mobile for this dribble. From the side Zack confuses the defender like this.

Zack is playing the ball forward with the outside of his right foot when he is confronted by a defender. Zack steps over the ball with his right foot and …

… immediately follows the right foot step over with a left foot step over.

Then with both feet on the right of the ball he quickly pushes off hard from his right foot and plays the ball left with the outside of his left foot.

The defender's utterly confused and well beaten.

From above the touches on the ball are as follows

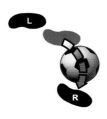

Step over with right foot.

Step over with left foot.

Explode away left.

From the front Zack feints as if he's going right twice, but he's gone left.

Zack sways right and steps over the ball with his right foot …

… and quickly follows up with a step over with his left foot.

Then explodes away left to beat the defender.

Tom's dribble

This is more of a trick than a dribble but it's particularly effective against onrushing opponents. Bruce Grobbelaar has used this trick before in a professional game, which is quite risky, but he did some famously crazy things anyway. Thierry Henry uses this trick successfully in attack. You telegraph the way you are going but the defender will expect the ball to move across the ground and will be surprised and beaten by the flick through the air into space. From the side Tom's trick works like this.

The ball is rolling just outside the penalty area, towards Tom, and an attacker is bearing down on him.	To keep the ball in play Tom flicks the oncoming ball over the outstretched leg of the attacker.	Tom is in the clear and can pass to a teammate or clear the ball safely up field.

From above the touches on the ball are as follows

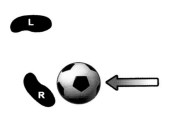 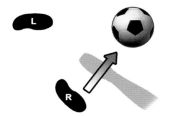 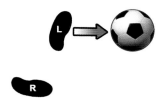

The ball rolls towards Tom.	Tom flicks the ball up and over the opponent.	Tom plays the ball into the open ready to pass.

From the front Tom beats the on rushing attacker like this

Tom judges it dangerous to kick the ball …	… so Tom flicks the ball up into the air over the opponent's legs.	Tom is clear to pass or kick.

Dribbling one v one game

Practise dribbling in a 1 v 1 situation to gain experience and learn which methods work well for you. In an area 15m long x 10m wide each end with a goal about 1.5m wide, place a ball in the middle and number the players so there are players 1 to 3 in this case on each side. Call a number and those two players should go for the ball and try to score a goal. The player not in possession can only jockey or block tackle, not dive in making physical contact.

Here Zack, Molly and Oscar are players 1, 2 and 3 on one side and Ryan, Jay and Katie are players 1, 2 and 3 on the other side.

The number one is called and Zack and Ryan rush out to get to the ball first.

Zack and Ryan dribble and jockey each other for ages but eventually Ryan manages to get clear and score.

Good effort from you both. Zack, your feints are becoming more convincing and your step overs, Ryan, are lightning quick.

Running with the ball

Running with the ball in open space to quickly attack uses a different technique from dribbling with the ball. To move quickly up field play the ball further in front of you so you can take several strides before playing the ball again. Try to play the ball without breaking your stride.

Contact zones

Contact is made with all areas of the forward part of your foot on the middle of the ball.

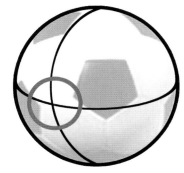

Contact on the ball is around the middle area. Slightly below the middle if you need to keep it moving over a muddy pitch.

The contact zone on your foot is either the **inside of the foot** or **outside of the foot** or **top of the toes** area, from your little toe to your big toe. Turn your toes in a generally downward direction.

Right foot running with the ball contact zone for touch with outside of foot and top of toes area. Little toe towards the ground and knee turned inwards.

Right foot running with the ball contact zone for touch with inside of foot and top of toes area. Big toe towards the ground and knee turned outwards.

Running with the ball technique

The type of touch on the ball will be determined by your stride pattern and where the ball is relative to the direction of your run. If the ball is running straight in front of you then the usual touch is to push the ball forward with the top of your foot near your little toe with your foot turned inwards and little toe towards the ground. Turn your knee in across your body as you touch the ball forward to make the leg action feel more comfortable and natural. If the ball is running wide of your desired direction of travel then bring it back on line with the inside of your foot.

When you get closer to opponents, change from running with the ball to dribbling and keep the ball under much closer control.

Keep your head up

Keep your head up so you can see the game around you and keep the ball in your peripheral vision as you move forward.

Molly is seen here running with the ball. She has good control and is aware of what's happening around her.

Running with the ball exercises

To a cone and back exercise

Run with the ball for about 20m, dribble round an obstacle and run back to the start.

Callum sets off quickly pushing the ball forward with the top of his toes. It's two or three strides before he touches it again. He uses the inside of his foot to get the ball round the cone.

Touch the ball every stride

To get more touches on the ball and improve your confidence when running with the ball try playing the ball forward at every stride, so that every time you lift your foot you play the ball. The ball must be kept close so you can touch it with your left foot then your right foot. Your touches must be gentle to succeed at this difficult exercise.

Callum is practising running with the ball by touching the ball forward at every stride.

From the front you can see Callum touching the ball forward with the outside of his right foot and then the inside of his left foot.

Callum's good at running with the ball.

If you can get a rhythm going touching the ball at every stride you will have the necessary skill to open up and run, touching the ball every few strides to move forward quickly.

TACKLING AND DEFENDING

Tackling an opponent while they have possession of the ball is the time when players are likely to be in physical contact. Because there is physical contact the tackling technique must be carried out correctly to ensure both players' safety. It is important to develop a good tackling technique.

Tackling is one element of football which can be taught in a formal way without stifling young players' initiative or flair. Correct tackling is a good practice to establish early. It helps reduce the chance of injury.

DEFEND THE GOAL AND REGAIN POSSESSION

When your opponents have the ball and are attacking your goal all your team is defending to win the ball back and prevent them scoring a goal. You can either **tackle** them and win the ball back or **defend** by pressurising them into making a mistake, which gives your team possession.

Before you can tackle or defend you have to be in the right position – goal side. You must always endeavour to be between your opponent and your own goal.

Tackling

Make a tackle only when you can get to the ball first without fouling an opponent.

The decision to tackle nearly always revolves around whether the opponent has got full control of the ball or not. In general if they haven't got full control close in and challenge. The exception to this is when they are shielding the ball with their body between you and the ball. If they have full control be wary and jockey them till you can get a foot to the ball without being beaten.

There are several types of tackle you can make on an opponent to win the ball.

Block tackle

When the ball is between you and the attacker you have a chance of winning and taking control of the ball directly.

The ball may be free and available to be won by either team and two players go for it at the same time in a '50-50' tackle. Turn your foot out at right angles to the ball and the other player and use your side foot just as with side foot control and kicking. Brace your body and make the tackle strongly and with conviction. Keep your eye on the ball when preparing and making the tackle.

Contact zone

Block the ball with the side foot. Put your side foot to the centre of the ball with the blocking foot off the ground just like a side foot pass.

Right foot block tackle contact zone.

Left foot block tackle contact zone.

It is important that you use your side foot and not your toes. Using the wrong part of your foot to block tackle could lead to twisted ankles and knee joints and damaged muscles.

Block tackling practise

Jay and Ryan place a ball between them and take one pace to plant their standing foot about 15cm to the side of the ball and with the tackling foot block the static ball in the middle simultaneously. The ball should remain static. Each player should feel comfortable after the tackle because the contact force should be resisted equally by the side foot, ankle, knee, hip and body.

Jay and Ryan practise side foot block tackling together so that when they do it for real they do it right and don't hurt themselves.

Step back and repeat the block tackle with the other foot. Repeat using alternate feet ten times or so. Practise this for only a short time so that your concentration does not wane.

Block tackle and come away with the ball

If you make a good 50-50 tackle and the ball is still close by maintain your challenge and keep touching the ball to win possession. For instance if the ball stays trapped between you and your opponents' feet try rolling the ball up and over your opponents' foot into the open so you can bring the ball away under control.

Zack makes a 50-50 block tackle on an attacker and when the ball gets trapped between their feet he quickly rolls the ball up over the attacker's right foot to get it clear.

Good skill, Zack. You've made a successful tackle and regained possession for your team.

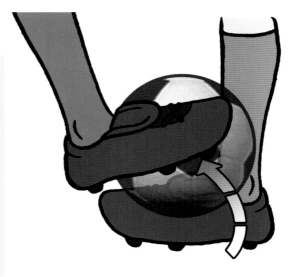

Tackle from the side

A defender running beside an attacker dribbling the ball forwards can make a tackle from the side. Timing the tackle is important because the attacker will be trying to touch the ball forward out of reach as the defender challenges for the ball.

The side on tackle is performed, as in the block tackle, with the side foot (inside of the foot).

Thus, if the defender is running on the right of the attacker, the tackle should be made with the right side foot and if the defender is running on the left of the attacker the tackle should be made with the left side foot.

Katie demonstrates the side on tackle from the right

Mary is running with the ball towards goal and Katie chases after her to jockey Mary away from goal.	As Katie gets alongside Mary she waits for her chance and under pressure Mary touches the ball a bit too far in front of herself.	And Katie seizes her opportunity to reach the ball first and play it to safety.

Notice how Katie running on the right beside Mary uses her right foot to make the tackle. This is the best way to tackle because you can get your right foot further across your opponent's body and if they fall on your legs your leg will bend in its natural direction so it's a safe technique as well.

Callum demonstrates the side on tackle from the left

In this next sequence Callum is jockeying Aiden from the left and makes his tackle correctly with, you've guessed it, his left foot.

Callum chases Aiden to challenge for the ball.	He pulls along side Aiden pressurising Aiden into temporarily losing control.	Callum confidently stretches his left leg out to clear the danger.

Sometimes your stride pattern means the other foot, the foot nearer the opponent, is better placed to make the tackle. C'est la vie. Seize the moment and make the tackle but immediately you've made the challenge protect your leg from being bent the wrong way.

Good tackling technique

It is both practical and safer to make any side on tackle with the side foot of the outside leg as shown above. It is practical because if you watch a professional match a right back running with a winger will prefer to tackle with his right foot and a left back will prefer to tackle with his left foot. It is safer because if the attacker falls forward onto the defender's leg after the challenge the leg can flex and there is much less chance of the ankle, knee and hip joints being injured.

Zack and Oscar demonstrate a poor tackle from the side

Here Zack is demonstrating a legal but unsafe way of tackling from the side. Oscar is running down the right wing and Zack makes the tackle with his right leg.

If Oscar fell awkwardly then Zack's leg, unable to flex, could be bent the wrong way and he could injure himself.

Zack and Oscar demonstrate a safe tackle from the side

Again Oscar is running down the right wing but this time Zack positions himself to win the ball with his left foot.

If Oscar fell over Zack then Zack's leg would flex safely under the pressure.

Zack can reach further round too, enhancing his chances of winning the ball cleanly. He could even pass the ball out of the tackle to a teammate.

Slide tackle

Another form of tackle is the **slide tackle** whereby the defender clears the ball, or wins control, by getting their body low and stretching out a leg while sliding on the pitch. Once the tackle is made the defender should get up as quickly as possible and regain a defensive position.

Contact zone

Contact may be with the top of the foot or ridge.

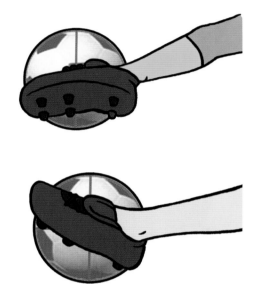

Contact may also be with the side foot.

This is a tackle of last resort performed when the attacker is closing in on goal and there is nothing else a defender can do to reach the ball.

Jay demonstrates the slide tackle

Good timing is important – too early and you may kick the attacker and give away a foul, too late and your chance to tackle may be lost.

Katie is running with the ball at her feet and Jay runs across to reach her before she shoots.

Jay lunges at the ball with his tackling leg, his other leg bends and collapses under him and he slides on the ground on his left buttock to reach the ball.

The ball may be kicked clear or held with your foot while the opponent overruns the ball.

Defending

When the attacker is in possession in space and you're not close enough to tackle you have to use other methods of defending your goal.

Defensive position

Primarily to defend, as in tackling, you have to be in the right position, which is goal side.

If you're defending against an opponent in any of these positions your primary objective is to get on the imaginary red line between the attacker and your goal, preferably tight on your opponent. You are now in a position to tackle or be part of a successful defence.

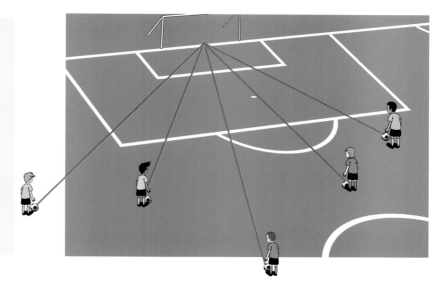

If you can't tackle them you must close them down to delay them and jockey them into losing control or making a poor pass. You might anticipate their pass and intercept it.

Jockey the attacker

Jockeying is a very important defensive skill. If an opponent gets the ball under control before you reach them you cannot rush in and try to tackle them because they will move the ball to the side and be gone. You must put pressure on them, close them down and shepherd them to a weaker position away from goal. This is called jockeying.

Oscar runs to get close to Katie who has just got the ball. He approaches quickly but slows down to a stop about 2m away. Oscar can't rush in to tackle because Katie will side step, push and go beyond him too easily.

When Oscar's close he half turns and offers Katie space to one side. He offers her the side he chooses, which will generally be the side away from goal. He then stays light on his feet, mobile and aware, ready to react quickly.

If the attacker is strong on one foot and weak on the other perhaps position yourself towards their stronger foot and make them play the ball with their weaker foot.

Even if the attacker doesn't try to get past you but passes the ball, make every effort to put pressure on the passer. Most players can make a good pass if they have time and space so when you're defending don't let them have time and space.

Deny the attacker space

If an opponent gets the ball with their back to your goal quickly deny them the space to turn. It is difficult for them to be creative and dangerous with their back to your goal.

The attacker will try and shield the ball from you.

In this situation Jay has placed himself between the attacker, Aiden, and the goal and is worrying Aiden into losing control.

Aiden is shielding the ball and Jay is looking for an opening to clear the ball. This is one part of the game where a toe poke (prodding the ball away with your toe end) would be useful because it gives the defender extra reach. The intention from Jay's point of view is to touch the ball away or force the attacker to lose control of the ball. The ball may then either go out of play or Jay's team may regain possession.

Remember you cannot tackle from behind or hold or push the attacker in the back with your hands but you're entitled to make your physical presence felt by getting in close. You must time any tackle so that you play the ball first. If the opponent is played before the ball then it will be a foul and the other team will get a free kick.

Intercept the pass

Tackling a player when they've got possession is one form of winning the ball but if a defender can anticipate when and where a pass is going then perhaps the pass could be intercepted. As you gain experience you will learn to anticipate a pass and judge whether you can reach it first and perhaps intercept it, thus winning the ball cleanly and being able to set up a quick counter attack.

Stay with your opponent and prevent possession

Be careful not to ball-watch and lose contact with the opponent you're defending against. If the player you're marking passes the ball don't follow the ball and forget your opponent. Stay with them otherwise they may get the ball back in an attacking position goal side of you.

For example the player you're marking may play a one-two with a teammate and run beyond you so you have to not chase the ball but stay with your opponent just like Katie. If you follow the ball your attacker will receive the return pass and be free on goal.

Katie demonstrates intercepting the pass

Katie is jockeying Aiden who is dribbling down the right wing. Aiden passes to Zack and runs beyond Katie for the one-two.

But Katie turns and stays with her attacker and intercepts the intended return pass.

Tackling one v one exercise

In an area about 10m x 5m wide with a small goal at one end players take turns to defend 1 v 1 against the other players. The defender tries to kick the ball out of the area to win a point. This gives varied practise against different styles of dribbling.

Molly starts off as the first defender about 5m in from the queue of attackers. Aiden is the first attacker and he dribbles the ball towards Molly and tries to get past her and score into the small goal.

Aiden can tap or dribble the ball into the goal but cannot shoot from distance.

Aiden keeps the ball under close control and tries to fool Molly with feints but she jockeys him to one side and closes him down until she can reach the ball and play it out of the area.

Molly's mobile and clever at defending.

Two to go, Molly.

Tackling one v the rest exercise

In an area about the size of the centre circle all the attackers have a ball each and the single defender tries to clear all the balls out of the circle. The attackers can dribble or shield the ball to make it difficult for the defender.

Oscar starts the exercise off and quickly clears the first ball out of the area before turning to tackle the other players in the circle.

Each player takes it in turns to be the defender and the time each player takes can be recorded. The winner is the defender who clears all the balls out of the circle quickest.

How to become a good defender

Be proactive and approach the act of tackling in such a way that your opponent feels worried and intimidated by your closing down and jockeying. Be patient and wait for an opening before making the tackle.

Make yourself difficult to get past

Get in position goal side, stay on your feet, well balanced, mobile and prepared to turn to either side, like Oscar, Jay, Katie and Molly. Try and impose your presence on the attacker to create doubt in their mind, perhaps feint to tackle and worry them into showing you the ball.

Don't make the attacker's mind up for them by over running the tackle.

Sam is not used to defending and here, when he runs back to tackle, he closes the attacker down too quickly and anticipates the direction the attacker will go.

The attacker, Molly, sees Sam go too far and turns back inside and clear.

Remember to jockey successfully, close them down and leave them no attacking outlet.

Use your eyes

Notice and be aware of what's going on around you. Regardless of where the ball is you should always know where the attacker you're marking is. Ball watching can give opponents too much space behind you on the blind side which they can exploit before you can get to them.

Teamwork

Stifle the attack by working with your teammates to reduce the space available for passing and receiving. Particularly look to cut off threatening passes into your penalty area.

Zack puts pressure on the attacker passing to her teammate who is running forward.

Aiden anticipates the pass and intercepts it to win possession.

Good team work and defending, you two.

Communicate

Help each other by talking. For instance talk to each other about runners off the ball or say which player you're going to mark so they know which one to go to. Listen for the central defenders calling for the team to push up and catch the opposition offside.

Know your opponent

Assessing your opponents' strengths and weaknesses gives you a chance to perform better against them. It's not something to analyse too deeply because that may frighten you and inhibit your own instinctive ability.

You may not have seen them play before, so early on in a match notice what the players you are likely to be up against do. They may be fast, tricky or strong and combative, be one-footed, good in the air, play-maker or individual. Make allowance to combat their strengths when you have to defend against them.

Where on the pitch is your opponent

Your approach to an attacker will vary depending where they are on the pitch. They may be in a dangerous position, inside your penalty area about to shoot, or still in their own half of the pitch creating no immediate threat.

If they are about to shoot on goal you must commit to a tackle even if there is a danger they will feint and step inside because in that case a second defender should be coming in to provide back up. Beware of the danger in your own area of making illegal contact with an opponent and giving away a penalty.

If they are in their own half close them down to pressurise them into making a poor pass but don't make a reckless tackle, which is unnecessary.

Defending at dead ball situations

At corners, free kicks, throw ins etc. keep your eye on the player you're marking and the ball in the corner of your eye at first. If your opponent gambles and runs before the kick, or throw, is taken then you must go with them. When you know where the ball is going, get to it first.

Defend at a corner

At this corner Jay can see the ball out of the corner of his eye but his gaze is firmly focused on the attacker he's marking.

When the ball is crossed he'll be able to challenge for the ball and won't be caught flat-footed.

When you've won possession

If you regain possession your next move depends on where on the pitch you've won the ball. You may be under severe pressure from the opposition near your own goal. Your only option may be to clear the ball into touch for a throw in or over the goal line (dead ball line) for a corner to relieve the pressure and make time for the defence to reorganise. You may only have enough time to turn and loft the ball clear, a long way up field.

If you are lucky and get the ball with time and space in a more forward position your good ball control and kicking ability should allow you to use it productively to set up your own team's attack.

Fouls, offences and breaches of the rules

Fouls can happen when you are playing football whether you're a defender or an attacker. Other offences or breaches of the rules, like hand ball or offside, can stop play and result in a free kick.

A **direct free kick** can be awarded for offences including:

- Deliberate hand ball
- Kicking an opponent
- Tripping an opponent
- Pushing an opponent

If the free kick is inside the penalty area a penalty kick is awarded. A goal can be scored from a direct free kick without anyone else touching the ball.

An **indirect free kick** can be awarded for several offences including:

- Playing in a dangerous manner, perhaps studs showing in an attempted tackle
- Interfering with play by impeding the progress of an opponent
- Being caught offside

A goal cannot be scored from an indirect free kick until a second player has touched the ball.

HEADING

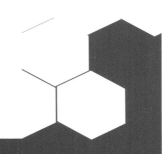

Playing with a ball on the ground often comes naturally at an early age but heading is a difficult skill to learn alone and doesn't always come naturally. You need confidence to be able to head the ball competitively. This confidence will only come once the techniques have been practised and honed. It is very satisfying to time a header and direct the ball to the target accurately.

Heading is best learnt in small groups as a fun activity where there is no pressure and the only objective is to make good contact with your forehead on the ball. Young players should practise heading technique regularly for a few minutes to build confidence and skill in preparation for playing games on full size pitches where heading is an integral part of the game.

Until sufficient physical maturity and co-ordination has developed it is safer for very young players to practise in a non-competitive heading environment.

Heading basics

Contact zone on your head

The contact zone on your head for most headers is the middle of the forehead just above the eyebrows. This is the solid and flat area of your head which helps you direct the header better.

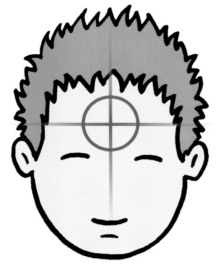

Here Callum shows us just where to make contact with the ball.

For glancing headers the contact zone may be to the right or left side of your forehead above the eyes. For flick-ons the contact zone is higher up towards the top of your head.

Get a feel for the ball

Start in a small group and practise for only a short time. Loop the ball to young players from about 2m to 3m or so. The intention is to get young players accustomed to the feel of the ball. Don't throw the ball hard and avoid throwing where two players compete for it. Use a ball appropriate for the age of the players, as you would for all aspects of football.

Tom, Jay, Katie and Callum are a bit older and used to the ball but it is still good for them to practise heading the ball back to the thrower.

Here the coach loops the ball underarm to each of them in turn so they can head the ball back using their forehead.

Timing, good contact and accuracy are what's wanted.

Nice one, Tom.

Try and head the ball and not let it head you. In other words control the ball, hit it with confidence and make a good follow through. With practise and experience you will be able to use your body, neck and head to generate power and distance.

Types of header

There are several different types of header. Depending whether the ball is looping to you or flying at you, or whether you're standing or jumping and whether it's a defensive or attacking header will determine which type you use and how you shape up to make contact with the ball.

Defensive Header

This is where the ball is cleared from the danger area by heading the ball out as far as possible. Keep your eyes on the ball and get in position under the ball to head it high and into space preferably towards the wing. The ball may go to an opponent but should take enough time to land for the defenders to push up and close the ball down.

Contact zone on the ball

The contact zone on the ball for a defensive header is just below the mid-point so it rises when you head it.

Zack demonstrates the defensive clearance

To defend against a high ball move to the line of flight of the ball, keep your eye on the ball and judge the timing of your leap so that you and the ball meet at the top of your jump. Use your arms for balance.

Zack is defending against Callum when a lofted pass comes high through the air.

They both jump for the ball …

… but Zack gets higher and seems to hang in the air ready to meet the ball. He uses his neck and upper body to balloon the ball back up field clear of danger.

Powerful clearance, Zack. Just like John Terry.

Attacking Header

Attacking headers are used most prominently for strikes on goal. They usually involve redirecting the ball into the net from a cross while under pressure from a defender. Attacking headers can also be used as passes in open play.

The type of attacking header on goal depends on whereabouts you are relative to the goal. You could be running in on goal towards the near post or jumping up at the far post. One way to understand the attacking header technique is to liken them to playing a side foot volley. If you were to side foot volley a ball at the far post back across goal you would use a short back lift and strike through the ball with a follow-through but if you were at the near post you would use virtually no back lift, redirect the ball with your side foot turned at an angle, and use no follow-through to find the net either at the far post or near post.

If you concentrate on making a good simple contact with your head on the ball to redirect it you will be surprised how fast it will go with little effort on your part.

Contact zone on the ball

The contact zone on the ball for an attacking header is just on or above the mid-point so the ball goes level or down towards the ground.

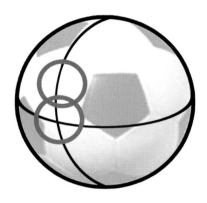

Callum demonstrates the attacking header

If you can, get above the ball so you can head it downwards towards the ground where the goalkeeper will find it difficult to save. Keep your eye on the ball and keep your header simple. Time your contact so you head the ball with your head, neck and back thrusting forward to power the ball towards goal.

Callum sees a cross flying towards his head so he takes one stride ….

… and sets himself to redirect the ball into the corner of the goal.

Fine header, Callum. What a good goal.

Near post header

To direct the ball towards the net from a cross to the near post you need to get the ball between you and the goal at the moment of contact. Contact on the ball is accurate rather than powerful. The degree of redirection will depend on the force and angle your head makes with the ball at the moment of contact. It sounds easy but it's a very difficult skill to learn. Alan Shearer was particularly good at changing the ball's direction and hitting the target with a simple movement of his head and good timing.

Zack sees a cross coming in from the left wing to the near post and runs to meet it. He judges the flight of the ball so he meets it at an angle when it arrives.

Zack turns his head to redirect it. He uses very little power or follow-through, just control so it will change direction and sail into the goal just inside the near post.

Top skill, Zack. Well judged and well executed.

Peter Crouch can jump at the near post and turn a cross into the net towards the far post with a well-timed turn of his head.

Far post header

A far post header is easier to execute than a near post header because you can get behind the line of the ball and direct it to any part of the goal. The ball is returned almost in the direction it came from with your forehead and the minimum of head turning. Use your neck and back to add power to your header.

Mary sees Katie dribbling down the wing and anticipates a cross to the far post.

Mary feints to go to the near post and doubles back to the far post leaving the defender stranded.

Katie sees Mary free and crosses pinpoint to Mary's head. As the defence turn to face the ball Mary heads it back across goal into the net at the far post.

You created good space and scored a quality goal, Mary.

Cushion control header

The cushion header is a difficult skill to master. But if the ball is coming to you too high to chest, you can use your forehead to cushion it to the ground. Get under the line of the ball and as the ball approaches flex your knees and hips and use your head to cushion it straight up in the air. Gravity will drop the ball at your feet. Put your hands out in front to balance your body.

Oscar sees a ball too high to chest and decides to control it with his head.

Oscar adjusts to the line of the ball. As the ball makes contact he leans back and yields and pops the ball straight up in the air.

The ball quickly comes straight down. Oscar adjusts his position and controls the ball with his foot.

That's exceptional skill, Oscar.

Glancing header

If you can't get in position to make a direct header to a teammate or at goal then you may be able to change the ball's direction by making a glancing contact with your forehead. A glancing header is difficult to direct accurately but it can create havoc for the defence. It could finish up in the net or it could lead to a teammate getting a goal scoring opportunity.

Emily gets up to a cross from the left wing but can't get in position to head at goal so she deflects the ball into the danger area so a teammate can challenge for it.

Flick-on

The flick-on is so called because you flick your head back to help the ball on its way usually to a strike partner. The ball skims off the top of your forehead.

Jay is under pressure from the defender and the ball is too high to control so he flicks it on with the top of his forehead for Oscar to run onto.

Challenge for the ball safely

There comes a time when two players will inevitably challenge for the same ball in the air and their heads will be very close. If there is a chance your face may be accidentally headed you can turn your face partially away but keep your eyes on the ball so you can still head it with part of your forehead. Be strong in the challenge and use your body and arms legally to hold the line of the flight of the ball then you will win the header.

Don't put your head in a situation where it could be kicked. It will hurt and is dangerous play. A foul will be given against you if you put your head too low onto the ball.

If you're old enough to get involved in challenging for a ball in the air you can use your arms to protect yourself, other players and win the ball. If you are on the line of flight of the ball you are entitled to shield your position using your arms to hold the other player off but you cannot elbow them or hold them down.

Zack is defending and jumping for the ball with Oscar. Their heads are very close, so to avoid a clash but still go for the ball, Zack turns his body and head slightly and, still with his eyes on the ball, heads it clear with the side of his forehead.

Heading practise

Solo heading keep ups

Stand in a large open space where you can't trip over and do keep ups with your head. Throw the ball in the air to get started.

Five headers is good. Ten is excellent. Above ten and you'll be like Alan Shearer.

You could also practise solo heading against a wall.

Heading in pairs exercise

This is a good heading exercise because you have to work together to make the heading easy for each other. See if you can keep it up so you do ten headers between you before the ball hits the ground.

Jay and Aiden practise heading together.

Jay throws the ball for Aiden to head it back – that's one.

Aiden and Jay head the ball backwards and forwards to each other. They adjust their bodies and stay mobile on their feet. They get up to twelve headers before the ball hits the ground.

Well done, you two.

Heading at goal exercise

Heading at goal can be practised safely with the coach throwing the ball under arm to each player in turn to replicate near post headers, far post headers and headers square on goal.

Here the team is practising near post headers.

The coach throws the ball to Zack who is ready to turn it into the goal at the near post.

Heading in groups exercise

Players can reproduce real match activities in groups to practise corners and crosses or free kick situations. Using just one goal and one goalkeeper take crosses from the left for a while and then change to take crosses from the right. In the middle are a group of defenders trying to clear the ball and a group of attackers trying to score.

It's like the real thing but with less intensity and pressure.

Agility exercise

To improve your timing, strength and to get more spring in your legs for jumping to reach headers, try skipping.

Skipping is excellent exercise for outfield players to help get extra height when jumping to head the ball.

Here Tom, the goalkeeper, also uses skipping to develop his leg muscles so he can spring off the ground to catch the ball.

GOALKEEPING

Goalkeeping involves a whole new range of handling and kicking skills. The handling skills involve saving the ball, parrying or deflecting the ball, catching the ball and throwing the ball. The goalkeeper's kicking armoury includes all the outfield ball control and kicking skills plus kicking the ball from hands, back pass clearances and goal kicks.

Goalkeeper training should cover the skills used by outfield players as well as the specialist handling and kicking skills.

Goalkeeper essentials

Goalkeeping is the most specialised position in the football team. The goalkeeper is the only player who can handle the ball in the penalty area during open play. Goalkeepers can see the play developing in front of them so they should command the penalty area in a positive way, both by their actions and verbally.

Goalkeeping can be quite hazardous and difficult for young players so care and tolerance are needed. Beginners are more prone to goal conceding mistakes, so be prepared to accept these mistakes calmly.

Goalkeeper kit

Good kit is essential. Padded gloves and tops with padded elbows provide protection to vulnerable joints. For hard grounds or in cold weather, long bottoms with padded knees make the goalkeeper's life easier. It may be a good idea for goalkeepers under twelve to wear protective headgear like Petr Čech.

Safety

Safety is an important matter for goalkeepers so throughout this section comments will be made about how to play safely. It's mostly a matter of common sense but do not lead with your head, remember goal posts are hard and so are football boots if they accidentally kick you. Be aware of what's going on around you so you can be properly prepared.

Be prepared

When an attack is building up a goalkeeper's primary objective is to be ready to react to any situation as it develops so read the situation, get in the right place in the goal and be in the prepared position.

The goalkeeper must concentrate and be prepared to save any shot.

Goalkeeping requires good balance, agility, mobility, being well positioned, relaxed and ready, and having fast reactions and speed of thought. Quite a list.

Tom the goalkeeper is in the prepared position.

On his toes, feet shoulder width apart, hands up, knees slightly bent and eyes on the ball.

From this prepared stance you should be able to jump, dive, move sideways or come forward easily.

Shot saving situations

Shots come in many guises. They can be high, low, fast, slow, dinked, chipped, bent, headed, deflected, close in, long range or dribbled into the net. Clearly goalkeepers have a lot to contend with.

Saves come in many varieties too, you can dive for a shot beyond arms length or you can jump for a high ball or to get above a crowd of players or you can move out to confront an attacker dribbling the ball, as well as many other situations.

Tom saves plenty of different shots when he practises with his teammates.

Tom dives to save a volley into the top corner of the goal from Ryan.

Jay chips the ball above Tom's head but he jumps just high enough to deflect it over the bar.

Tom saves bravely at Zack's feet as he attempts to dribble round the goalkeeper.

Here Emily jumps high to hold the ball just below the crossbar.

Tom clutches a bullet shot from Emily to his chest and cups his hands to hold the ball.

Tom moves across the goal and takes a low shot safely into his arms.

Callum's blistering drive into the bottom corner brings a great save from Tom.

Katie wants to dribble the ball in but Tom moves out to narrow the angle. Will Katie score?

Sam bends a shot which deceives Tom but he reacts to deflect the shot after initially going the wrong way.

Oscar powers a drive near the post but Emily dives full length to deflect the ball round the post.

The team practises corners and Tom bravely jumps in the crowd of players to take the ball safely.

Mary dribbles in and tries a side foot shot close to Tom's body but he quickly sticks his leg out and clears the ball with his foot.

Catching and Holding the Ball

Catch a shot above chest high

Keep your eyes on the ball, hands close together, palms facing the ball with fingers spread and pointing up and wrists strong.

| Tom is preparing to jump for the high ball with his knees slightly bent. | Tom leaps into the air with arms out-stretched ready to catch the high ball with both hands. | He takes it securely with both hands gripping the ball and as he returns to the ground. | Tom slides his hands under the ball to bring it safely into his chest or stomach. |

Holding the ball

When you can get both hands to a high ball keep your hands close enough together to stop the ball slipping between them but far enough apart to get a good grip so it sticks when it hits your hands.

Tom catches the ball with his fingers spread out and pointing up.

He takes the ball securely in both hands.

Catch a shot below chest high straight to the body

If you can get behind the line of travel of the ball as it is struck, bend your knees to suit the height of the ball and take the ball in your midriff or chest. Your body should cushion the shot. Wrap your hands quickly around the ball with your palms facing up.

Tom gets behind the line of the ball and positions himself to get the ball safely into his midriff with his arms cupped under the ball and holding it on impact.

Cushion the ball to reduce its energy. It's harder to cushion the ball with your chest than your stomach so beware the ball doesn't just bounce off you before your hands get behind it. Remember to keep your eyes on the ball all the time.

Saving a straight shot

If a shot comes near you on the ground get your whole body behind the line of the ball and take it securely in your hands. Beware of the ball bouncing cruelly off the pitch past you.

Tom sees a shot on target but along the ground and has time to move sideways, get behind the line of the ball and bend down on one knee to take the ball safely in his hands. His hands are close together and palms facing out. His legs are close together as well so the ball can't get through the gap.

Challenging for a high ball

A goalkeeper sometimes has to jump for a high ball while being challenged by an attacker.

In this practise Katie crosses the ball close to goal and Oscar jumps to challenge for the ball but Tom has the advantage because he can jump and reach up above Oscar's head to catch the ball in both hands.

As players get older, corners and crosses become more demanding and goalkeepers need to be brave and confident in a crowded penalty area.

Diving for the ball

Diving full stretch

Move quickly across the goal to get in line with a shot to make a straightforward save if possible but if you can't then get across as far as you can before diving. When you make a dive rock sideways towards the shot and push off from the leg nearest to the ball to get lots of spring. Your legs should be slightly bent at the knees initially.

Dive with your body sideways (not facing the ground) and reach out with your arms slightly in front of you and your hands close together. Spread your fingers out to give a large area to make contact with the ball. Catch the ball with both hands and hold onto it and if you have time get the ball tucked in so you can cushion your landing with your arm and body.

Tom rocks sideways from the prepared position and is about to leap to intercept the ball.

Here you can see Tom diving full stretch sideways. He takes the ball in the air with his arms out in front and hands close together holding the ball securely.

Tom dives full stretch to save a low wide shot

Sam and Tom are practising shooting and saving shots together.

Sam runs into the penalty area with the ball under control at his feet.

Before the shot Tom can be seen, from close up, getting himself ready on his toes with knees slightly bent and hands up.

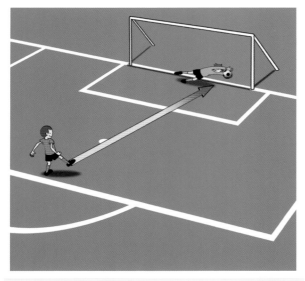

Sam drives the ball to Tom's left but Tom reacts instantly, pushing off from his left leg and stretching his arms out.

From close up, Tom gets both hands behind the ball and holds the shot. He pulls the ball in and lands with it safely.

Well held, Tom.

Diving for a shot close to the goalkeeper

High shot close to goalkeeper

If the shot is close to you and high so you don't have to dive far, rock sideways or dive to get your body behind the line of the ball. Get your arms out in front of you, bent at the elbows and hands close together, just like the high ball catch, and take the ball safely. You will have time to land safely on your upper arm and side with your elbows off the ground keeping the ball free of jolts.

Tom dives for a shot close to his body. After he takes the ball in the air he will pull it to his body and land on his upper arm and body.

Tom's forearm will not touch the ground so the ball is held safely.

Low shot close to goalkeeper

If the shot is low and close to your feet and you haven't got time to dive, you have to drop on it or perhaps kick at it. To drop on the ball rock sideways with your arms reaching for the ground, bend your knees, allow your feet to slip out from under you and let your body fall onto the ball quickly.

Here is a close up from the front showing Tom getting down to the ball.

His knees are bent so he can fall to the ground quickly.

Tom saves a low shot close to him

Ryan is practising dribbling towards goal and shooting from close in.

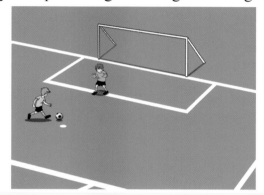

Ryan has virtually the whole goal to aim at but Tom sees the danger and steps forward with arms held up in the ready position.

As Ryan strikes the ball to the goalkeeper's left Tom quickly bends his knees and collapses onto the ball clasping it to his chest.

You got down quickly to make that save, Tom.

Diving at feet

When diving at the feet of an attacker coming straight at you spread your body out flat and put your arms out in front bent at the elbow and hands close together with fingers spread out. Take the ball with strong wrists and hands and then clasp it to your body. This is the best way to protect the goal and is the safe way to protect yourself.

From the front you can see Emily spread herself at the oncoming attacker's feet and take the ball cleanly.

Emily wears protective headgear when she plays in goal.

Never dive head first at the attacker's feet with your head exposed to accidental kicks.

Tom saves bravely from Zack

Here we can see Tom saving at Zack's feet from behind the goal.

Zack dribbles from outside the penalty area and Tom moves out to narrow the angle and sees Zack has kicked the ball too far ahead. Tom seizes the opportunity and runs towards the ball.

Tom dives and spreads himself out in front of the ball and gathers it to his chest.

Zack avoids the clash because he's lost his chance of getting to the ball first.

There may sometimes be contact between keeper and attacker so the keeper must be careful to get the ball first and avoid giving away a penalty.

Attackers must be made aware to pull out of the challenge if the keeper gets control of the ball first. Attackers cannot tackle a goalkeeper in full possession of the ball.

Land safely

When you dive, whether you hold the ball or deflect it, always land safely and cushion your impact with the ground. Try to land on a combination of your arm and side of your body not on your elbows, wrists, stomach or knees. If you dive for a high ball you may have a chance to tuck your arms into your body cushioning the landing and holding the ball securely.

If you can't get the ball tucked in land on your outstretched arms and body together keeping your hands and the ball clear of the ground if possible.

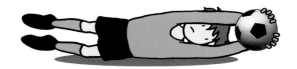

Tom makes a good diving save from a high shot and has time to tuck his arms and the ball into his body safely cushioning the landing. Tom keeps his forearm and the ball off the ground.

Here Tom has dived low and has to use his outstretched arm and body to help cushion his landing. Notice how he uses his upper arm and forearm together to help cushion the landing.

Deflecting shots

Tip a high shot over the bar

Keep your eyes on the ball. If you can get to the line of the ball use both hands but if not use the hand closest to the ball. In both cases stretch with fingers spread and pointing up and wrists strong.

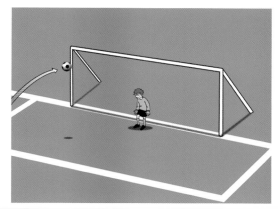

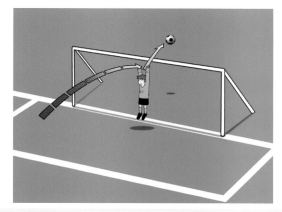

This long shot from Aiden is on target but too high for Tom to catch …

… so Tom jumps and times his leap so that at full stretch he can tip the ball over the bar.

Tip a wide shot around the post

If a wide shot comes in and you can only dive and parry it try and push it wide away from danger and not back into play in front of goal. Again use the hand nearer the ball. Usually if the ball is high use your upper hand as you dive sideways and if the ball is low use your lower hand as you dive sideways.

Molly strikes a fast low drive just inside the far post….

…but Tom makes a brilliant dive to get his finger tips to it and deflect it out of play for a corner.

How did you manage to reach that shot, Tom?

Here Tom is practising with Katie. Katie dribbles the ball into the penalty area.

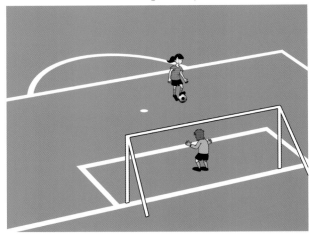

Tom steps forward to reduce the size of the target and prevent Katie coming close and stands tall, trying to put doubt into Katie's mind about her chances of scoring.

Katie sees more space at the far post so she drives her shot across the goalkeeper just inside the post to beat the goalkeeper to his left but Tom pushes off the ground hard with his left leg and stretches to tip the ball beyond the post.

Excellent save, Tom. You showed fast reactions and good coordination to save that shot.

Saving with your feet

If an attacker shoots and the ball travels on the floor close to you it may be impossible to get your body down to the ball quickly enough with your hands so use a leg or foot to block it.

Jay has been put through on goal with the ball at his feet but before Tom can get close Jay drives it low to Tom's right. Tom reacts quickly and lunges his right foot out to deflect the shot past the post. Tom's left knee is bent across his body to prevent the ball getting under him.

Positional Play

Movement

Goalkeepers patrol the whole penalty area during a game but when the other team is attacking in numbers you are likely to be on the goal line between the goal posts or a metre or so in front of the goal line ready to react. As the attack switches direction you should move quickly across the goal to mirror the position of the ball. Your movement across the goal should be a balanced sideways shuffle like a crab without your feet crossing. In this way you will always be prepared for a snap shot and not be caught off balance with your legs crossed.

Reduce the target

One of the main skills of a goalkeeper is to make the goal look small to an attacker and make them indecisive about their shot. A goalkeeper can make the goal look small by coming off the goal line to confront the attacker. This is known as 'narrowing the angle'. The goalkeeper's position is on the imaginary line from the ball to the centre of the goal. The distance along the imaginary line depends on the situation but in a one-on-one the closer to the attacker the better.

If the goalkeeper stays on the line then there is a large area of goal, seen here in red, he cannot easily defend.

This time in the same situation Tom comes off his line and immediately the area of goal available to hit for the attacker is reduced.

The red area is smaller.

Narrow the angle

Here we can see the stages Tom goes through to narrow the angle and close the available space for a shot. As Aiden closes in from outside the penalty area Tom moves out to confront him. Tom comes out carefully along the imaginary line linking the ball to the centre of the goal ready to react at any moment. He can't come too far because Aiden could chip the ball over him into the net but Tom's gradually closing the space down.

Tom must be aware of where the goal posts are so he can be on the imaginary line. Tom must also stand tall and intimidating for as long as possible and react quickly when the attacker kicks the ball.

Tom is ready on the goal line and sees Aiden running with the ball at goal from outside the penalty area. Tom must put pressure on the attacker and intimidate him into making a mistake so he moves off the goal line to reduce the space available for Aiden's shot to get past him into the goal.

Aiden gets into the penalty area but sees Tom standing tall with arms out making the goal look small. Aiden can't wait any longer because they're getting too close together and defenders are chasing back to help so he shoots across the goalkeeper to the far post. But Tom dives and saves the ball because he has moved out to "narrow the angle" and given himself a good chance of reaching the ball.

Throwing the Ball

If the keeper has the ball in hand there are several throwing options to keep possession and start a penetrating counter attack

Throw under arm

To cover a short distance direct to a teammate use an underarm roll out. This pass is usually along the ground to make it easier for the receiver to control and turn to face up field.

Tom throws it firmly and times the release to make the ball run smoothly over the ground.

Throw over arm

To cover a longer distance into open space use an over arm throw out. Keep the arm straight and move swiftly to the point of release.

This is a good counter attacking throw, up field, for a teammate to run onto, so get the weight of the throw right.

Spear throw

Tom uses this throw to clear opponents close to him.

Hold the ball at shoulder height and push it hard to a teammate in space just outside the penalty area.

Small hands will find throwing difficult unless the correct size small football is used. A large ball may slip sideways out of the goalkeeper's grip.

Remember that once in hand the ball can be held for only six seconds but you can use the whole penalty area to move around before releasing it if you want.

Kicking the Ball

Once a save has been made you may want to clear the ball far down the pitch.

Volley from hands

Tom uses the volley from hands to achieve height and distance. This should safely clear the opposition attackers. It is the least accurate clearance but covers the greatest distance with least risk.

Throw the ball slightly up into the air to give yourself time to volley it. Kick the ball with the top of your foot before it touches the ground so your foot gets under the ball. Keep your eye on the ball at the moment of contact.

Half volley from hands

Tom occasionally uses the half volley from hands to cover distance quickly. It stays low for a time and could be dangerous if intercepted by the opposition so Tom only uses it if the space in front of him is clear. Make contact with the ball with the top of your foot or ridge just as it touches the ground.

This is a trickier skill than the volley from hands.

Kicking from a back pass

If a defender kicks the ball back to the goalkeeper he cannot pick it up but must kick it. Goalkeepers are becoming more involved in this type of open play and they must be able and confident in their ability to clear the ball up field. So the ball skills learned with the outfield players are very useful.

Here Tom has moved out to help his fellow defenders. The ball is passed back to him and he moves out to meet it.

Tom has practised ball control and kicking a lot and feels relaxed about the back pass.

Tom makes contact below the centre of the ball with the top of his foot or the ridge and sends it into the air upfield over the oncoming opponents. Good timing, Tom.

Keep your eye on the ball and beware of the ball bobbling over your foot at the last moment.

Ball handling practise

Practise handling the ball to improve feel and gain confidence. Here are some of the exercises you can do. All players should take part in these activities.

Round the body

Pass the ball from hand to hand in a circular motion around your body. It is good ball handling practise and helps coordination and concentration. Practise moving the ball clockwise and anti-clockwise.

Figure of eight

With feet apart and legs bent a little pass the ball from hand to hand in a figure of eight between your legs. It is good for agility and confidence. Again repeat the exercise clockwise and anti-clockwise.

Hand to hand

Pass the ball from hand to hand in front of your body. Again both hands become accustomed to catching, manipulating and moving the ball on.

Throw out

Practise throwing the ball out but don't let go, throw it to the palm of your other hand. Then use your other hand so both hands get to handle the ball.

Here Tom is throwing the ball from his right hand to his left. Once the ball is in his left hand he'll throw it to his right hand and so on.

Bounce and catch

Bounce the ball hard on the ground either with one hand or both hands so it bounces straight up in the air and catch it safely as it comes down.

Goalkeeper exercises

Throw and catch

Ryan and Katie are about 5m apart, throwing the ball to each other.

All the players practise catching, handling and throwing the ball.

It improves coordination and movement.

Throw and catch with two balls

Tom and Jay with two footballs practise throwing and catching.

Following a throw instantly with a catch makes for fast hand movements and quick reflexes.

Throw and catch against a wall

Aiden throws the ball against a wall and catches it on the rebound.

He's getting into the good habit of moving to get his body behind the line of the ball before he catches it.

Kick and save against a wall

Tom kicks the ball against a wall and saves it on the rebound.

He sometimes kicks it high and sometimes low to force himself to make different types of save.

One to one saves

Tom and Oscar are about 5m – 8m apart with Oscar kicking the ball for Tom to save. Oscar plays different types of kick, left, right, low and high for Tom to practise.

Oscar sometimes kicks the ball from his hands so Tom can practise saving volleys.

Throw out exercise

During shooting practise it can be set up so the goalkeeper gets throwing out practise too. A quick throw out can catch the opposition too far up field and start a successful counter attack.

When the goalkeeper saves the ball it should be thrown out to the coach who is standing at any one of three cones. Each cone is positioned to require a different throw out pass. The coach should return the ball to the striker.

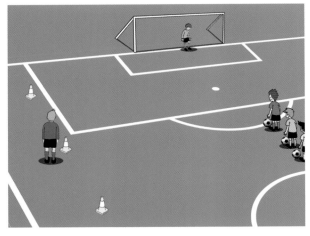

During a dribble and shoot attacking routine the coach introduces a variation where if Tom saves a shot he must throw it out to the coach.

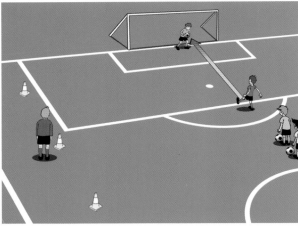

Zack takes his turn to shoot on goal but his shot is well saved by Tom.

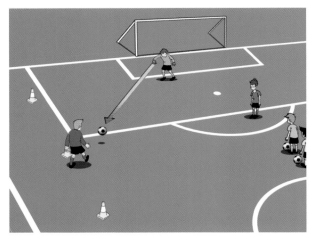

Tom turns with the ball in hand and sees the coach at cone two.

Tom takes a couple of paces and throws the ball overarm to the coach's feet.

A good throw to keep possession and start a quick counter attack.

The coach can position the cones on either wing so the throw out can be to wide left or wide right.

Goalkeeping and the rules of the game

Goal kick

If an opponent kicks the ball over the dead ball line away from the goalposts or over the crossbar, it's a goal kick.

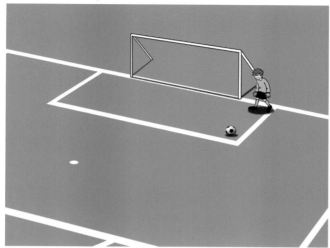

The goalkeeper, or a teammate, can restart the game by placing the ball anywhere in the six yard area and kicking it into play. The ball must go beyond the penalty area before it is in play. It can then be touched by any player.

To clear the ball a long way up field Tom would probably use a lofted drive.

Penalty

If the defending team concedes a direct free kick inside their penalty area it's a penalty to the attacking team.

The only two players allowed inside the penalty area and the D, before the kick is taken, are the defending goalkeeper and the penalty taker. The goalkeeper can move sideways and 'wobble', à la Bruce Grobbelaar, to distract or put off the penalty taker but can only move to make the save after the penalty taker has kicked the ball.

All the other players from both teams have to be at least ten yards away from the penalty spot until the ball is kicked. Hence the purpose of the D, which is part of a circle ten yards, radius from the penalty spot.

Goalkeeper offences

Several goalkeeper offences result in indirect free kicks inside the penalty area including:

- Handling the ball from a throw in direct from a teammate
- Handling the ball from a deliberate kicked backpass from a teammate (a headed backpass from a teammate or backpass using any other part of the body, like chest or thigh is ok)
- Holding the ball for more than six seconds

PLAY COMPETITION FOOTBALL

If you want to play competitive 11 a-side football you'll need a pitch, two teams and a referee. To play in a league you will need to join a club affiliated to a local league.

You can also play in small sided games like organised 5 a-side or 7 a-side leagues at sports centres and outside pitches.

Junior Clubs & Competition

If you have access to the internet one easy way of finding Football Association (FA) affiliated clubs in your area is to go on the FA website **thefa.com**.

Click on the icon '**grassroots**' in the website home page then click on the label '**find a club**' and enter your postcode and the distance you are willing to travel. All the affiliated clubs within that travelling distance will appear. The age groups that the clubs run and the local league they play in will be shown. You can then phone their contact or visit them to find out whether it's the right club for you. Alternatively you can talk to school friends, find out who they play for, and join their team or visit a local club in your area, find out the name of the team manager for your age group and talk to them. They should be happy to let you train with them to see if it's what you want.

Have an idea of what you play football for. Is it to train and compete hard or is it more to keep fit and be sociable. Some clubs are run on a friendly basis where the result isn't everything but others are more competitive. The manager, coach and players work hard to come first. Whichever type of club you want there should be one available locally to suit your needs.

If you want to learn the techniques and skills of football check that the team has got a knowledgeable coach.

The website **thefa.com** is full of other useful information about football from the Premier League downwards. For information about grassroots local leagues, fixtures, results and league tables click on **thefa.com/FULL-TIME**.

Guidelines, Laws and Regulations

If you are serious about joining a club or league it helps to know the laws governing the game. There are many variations on the basic game of football played and many rules govern young age group games. Players under 18 are organised into age groups so that players compete with their contemporaries only. This is simply to recognise that children progress physically and mentally as they mature.

Again the FA website thefa.com is very useful. It contains information on the rules, regulations and laws of the game for 11 a-side games, small sided games or mini soccer games. It will tell you details about the pitch size and markings, the ball, number of players, player equipment, referees and duration of the games.

Types of football games

For young players from seven to ten years of age the FA recommend Mini Soccer, a simplified game for sides 4v4 or 5v5 at under eight (U8) up to 7v7 at U10. From U11 to U18 full games of eleven a side may be played. The definition of U10 for example varies from league to league but generally a player is under ten for the coming season if they are still nine prior to a fixed date, usually in August. The player can have their tenth birthday at any time during the season after the fixed date.

At U12 and older, girls and boys usually cannot play competitively together.

Football pitch

For U7 and U8 mini soccer the pitch is between 30 to 50 yards long by 20 to 30 yards wide. For U9 and U10 mini soccer the pitch is between 50 to 60 yards long by 30 to 40 yards wide. For youth football at U11 to U17 the pitch is between 75 to 90 yards long by 45 to 60 yards wide. After U17 football is open aged and played on full-size pitches.

The diagram below shows half a full-size pitch layout with the common terms for the pitch line markings and areas.

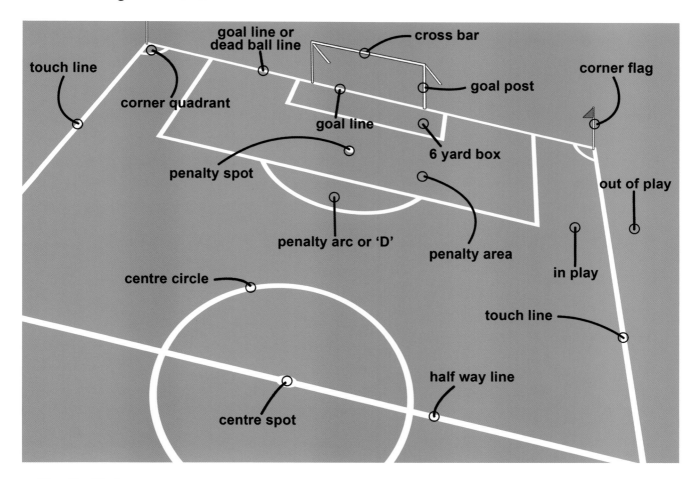

Football sizes

The size of football used should get bigger to reflect the increasing age and size of the players. The football for players U8s should be a size 3, for age groups up to U12s the ball should be size 4. For U13s and over the adult size 5 football should be used.

Some laws of the game

Ball in or out of play

Law 1 of the rules of the game states that the lines marking out a football pitch are part of the field of play so the ball is in play unless the whole ball has crossed a touch line or goal line like this.

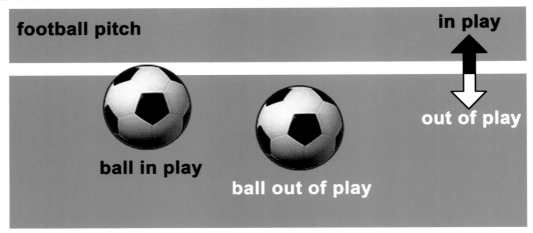

If the ball goes out of play over either touch line it's a throw in and if the ball goes out of play over the goal line (dead-ball line) it's a goal kick or corner.

Of course if the ball crosses the goal line between the goal posts it's a goal.

Corner kick

Corner kicks are covered by Law 17. If the defending team touches the ball out over its own dead-ball line, the game is restarted with a corner kick to the attacking team. The corner kick is taken with the ball static inside the quadrant.

The corner flag must remain in position at all times during the game.

Just like the lines marking the boundary of the pitch the lines marking the corner quadrant are part of the quadrant.

The ball in this picture is within the quadrant because it is not fully beyond the line. It is legal according to the rules of the game as long as part of the ball is overhanging the line.

Offside

Law 11, covering the rules for offside, has become more complex in recent years but in general an active player (the player about to receive possession) is **offside** if they are in the opponent's half of the pitch with fewer than two opponents between them and the goal when the ball is passed forward to them by a teammate.

To be **onside** you need two opponents, one is usually, but not necessarily, the goalkeeper, between you and the goal if you are the active player in your opponent's half when the ball is passed forward to you. Other players could be in an offside position but not active; that is not participating in this particular attack.

Zack and Mary are standing in offside positions but not actively involved in this attack so they are not committing an offence.

Molly had Tom and Callum between her and the goal when she set off running after Jay passed to her. Molly is **onside** and can continue her lone attack.

It's worth noting you can't be offside from a goal kick, corner or throw in, so get beyond the opposition and take advantage of these rules if the opportunity arises. You are also onside if a teammate passes the ball back to you from a more forward position.

If a player is caught offside the referee will award an indirect free kick.

Match official signals

Referee signals

The most common hand signals a referee or referee's assistant will make are the following:

Direct free kick

Indirect free kick

Advantage play on

Goal kick

Corner kick

Penalty kick

Yellow card caution

Red card sending off

Referee assistant signals

Throw in

Substitution

Offside

Offside
1. Farside
2. Middle
3. Near

Preparation for a match

The **technical skills** presented in this book are the foundation for your chances of winning a competitive game of football. But alongside those technical skills, **team formation and tactics** should be added. An experienced coach or manager usually chooses the team formation and tactics.

On match day **warm up** before the game. Start slowly and gently to loosen up with gentle stretching and jogging exercises. Then move on to loosen up with kicking, passing and moving exercises. Finally extend yourself with short sprints and perhaps a small-sided game for a few minutes. The intention is to get your body and mind ready to go as soon as the competition starts but not make yourself tired. In winter keep a warm, easy to remove, tracksuit over your kit until near the kick off.

Warm down at the end of a match by repeating the gentle stretching and jogging for several minutes or longer if possible. This helps reduce muscle fatigue.

Health, fitness and diet

In football, as in other sports, there are other aspects of health, like **physical fitness and diet**, which help you not only become a better player but a healthier person. Generally a balanced diet and the rigorous exercise you'll get playing football and training will help you keep healthy and happy.

Behaviour

How you conduct yourself on and off the playing field is an important part of the game. Play hard but fair and always to the best of your ability.

Treat the referee and other players with respect. They are all doing their best, just like you.

It is good to win and nobody enjoys losing but either way try to be cool. If you can outwardly appear to be modest in victory and gracious in defeat you will get the respect of everyone.

Above all remember that football is fun and the most important thing is that you enjoy it.

ACKNOWLEDGEMENTS

With thanks to

Julie Ashworth, Ian Emmott, Bethany Gardner, Steve Green, John Palliser
John Pease, Karen Phillips, Paulene Rossiter, Chris Sugden, John Wilkes

For proof reading, technical input, suggestions and help.